50 GREATS

BRISTOL BULLDOGS
SPEEDWAY

50 GREATS
BRISTOL BULLDOGS
SPEEDWAY

ROBERT BAMFORD
&
GLYNN SHAILES

TEMPUS

First published 2003

Tempus Publishing Limited
The Mill, Brimscombe Port,
Stroud, Gloucestershire, GL5 2QG

British Library Cataloguing in Publication Data.
A catalogue record for this book is available from the British Library.

ISBN 0 7524 2865 9

Typesetting and origination by Tempus Publishing Limited
Printed in Great Britain by Midway Colour Print, Wiltshire.

Foreword

There was something very special about Bristol Speedway, and Knowle Stadium, both before and after the Second World War. Not only were patrons treated to top-class racing, week in, week out, but no sooner had you passed through the turnstiles, there was an extra buzz about the place. Everything about the sport at Knowle was special, the post-war team were all local boys, having either moved to, or been born in, the area and they weren't just riding heroes either, as they seemed like members of your very own family. Even the notes in the Bristol programme, penned in the pre-war days by Ronnie Greene, and after the hostilities by Reg Witcomb, and then George Allen, read like a personal letter written by your favourite Aunt or Uncle.

Bristol had built teams that earned promotion by their own riders on-track efforts. The first occasion was in 1938, after they had won the previous season's Provincial League Championship. It was a just reward for a lot of hard work, and the Control Board saw to it that the four riders of Division One status were allocated to the side in order to bring them up to strength. How proud Supporters' Club member no.1289 must have been, when his local club, having assumed the 'Bulldogs' nickname at his behest, had achieved top-flight status. Sadly, it wasn't to last, as Bristol ended the year receiving the wooden spoon. Nevertheless, the Knowle regulars had doubtless enjoyed watching American Cordy Milne, and the 'Great Dane' Morian Hansen in action. Cordy was certainly one of the best riders to ever wear the club's famous orange and black colours, and it was indeed a proud occasion when as a Bulldogs rider, he raced in the 1938 World Final at Wembley Stadium.

After the war, Bristol attracted huge crowds, and the team of local boys did the City proud. Following a season of open-licence events in 1946, and a year of settling down to Division Two league racing in 1947, the Bulldogs went on to Championship glory in 1948. Having failed to be awarded a place in the higher league, for good measure, they went and won the Division Two title again in 1949. It was overdue, but they were finally awarded promotion to Division One, however, this time there was no help forthcoming from the controlling body in the form of rider allocations. This was a shock to all concerned with the club, but it did enable Bristol to find, and train their own stars, whilst all the time being unfairly tagged as 'unfashionable'.

Perhaps the brightest shining star, and a rider who really made fans sit up and take notice, was Dick Bradley. He went from strength-to-strength as a Bulldog, reaching the World Final as reserve in 1951, and the meeting proper in 1952. Dick rose to become Bristol's leading rider, although he will probably be best remembered for his England Test match debut at Harringay in 1952, when from the reserve berth, he plundered 16 points, and helped his country to a 55-53 victory over Australia. From that moment on, both Bristol and Dick Bradley were well known, although there is little doubt that had he, Jack Mountford, and long-time Bristol skipper Billy Hole, ridden for a more 'fashionable' side during the 1950s, they would have received honours a plenty. But the boys were loyal, they only wanted to ride for the Bulldogs and that's where they were content to stay.

Sadly, in the 1950s, speedway was on something of a descending spiral, and Bristol closed down mid-way through the 1955 campaign. However, a brand new venture saw the sport resume at Knowle, initially on an open licence in 1959, prior to the entering of a team in the newly formed Provincial League a year later. The Bulldogs were led in the new league by long-time clubman Johnny Hole, plus local boy Cliff Cox, and the experienced Trevor Redmond, whose previous teams included the mighty Wembley. How good it was to hear the roar of the speedway bikes again at Knowle Stadium, and the crowds simply flocked through the gates. Sadly, it was not to last, and on 23 January 1961 came the news that the stadium had been sold, and Bristol Bulldogs were no more.

They did make a return to the track in 1977, however, but not at Knowle Stadium (which had long since become a housing estate), instead racing at Eastville Stadium, the then home of

Bristol Rovers FC. The speedway at Eastville was 'different' to say the least, but the supporters packed the arena each week, with the Bulldogs enjoying the very best crowds in the sport, until they were closed down after the 1978 season had ended.

Throughout the years since Bristol first rode as a team in 1936, the club were privileged to have been served by many heroes of the track. It is the pleasure of Robert Bamford and myself to pay tribute to 50 of them here. All of these lads served the club well, and earned the plaudits of the loyal supporters. We hope that your particular favourite is included here and that this book will bring back a host of happy memories of Bristol Speedway, and the 'gladiators' who made it all possible.

Glynn Shailes
July 2003

Acknowledgements

Acknowledgement is made to Mike Craven for his wonderful article on Fleetwood in *The Speedway Researcher*, which greatly helped to augment the piece on Mike Beddoe. Grateful thanks are due to Matt Jackson for his invaluable assistance with dates and places of birth for various riders, and also to Dick Bradley for taking the trouble to clarify his own details. Much gratitude is also due to the amazing George Craig, who was only too pleased help clear up one of speedway's long-term misconceptions, which has always incorrectly identified Bristol as his birthplace. To the genial Tony Lethbridge, much appreciation is due for information on the late Jack Unstead, which was gleaned from his marvellous book *The Story of Exeter Speedway 1954-1964*. We also acknowledge the excellent Tempus publication *Hackney Speedway – Friday At Eight* by Chris Fenn, which proved to be source of additional snippets of information in creating the profiles on Bill Clibbett, Vic Duggan, Morian Hansen and Cordy Milne. Thanks also go to old friend Keith Farman in Great Yarmouth for coming up with invaluable information on both Fred Leavis and Roy Taylor. As ever, the amazing John Jarvis has provided the answers to numerous questions at the drop of a hat, as well as supplying much of this book's content, through his vast collection of Bristol memorabilia. To the ever-obliging Tony Jackson up in Workington, a big 'thank you' for helping to augment the Rol Stobart story. The speedway press too, has been a constant source of information over the years and to this end, we would like to express our gratitude to various magazines namely, *Speedway World*, *Speedway Echo*, *Speedway News*, *Speedway Star*, *On The Track*, *The Motor Cycle* and *Broadsider*. Mention must also be made here of the excellent series of *Speedway Archives* publications by Peter Jackson, which have proved to be a wonderful point of reference. As ever, no book would be complete without photographs, and to this end, the authors acknowledge the excellent images from F. Fowler, Wright Wood, J.P.B. Shelley, Stan Vicars, Ralph Jackson, C.F. Wallace, T.H. Everitt, Alf Weedon, and the wonderful collection of Geoff Parker.

Introduction

Bristol Speedway is very special to me, since it was at Knowle Stadium on 18 July 1947, that I saw my first-ever meeting. However, I didn't attend the Bulldogs British Speedway Cup match against Wigan with a view to seeing any riders in action. On the contrary, as a choirboy, I had visited Bristol that day to look around the cathedral – and to see Hollywood stars Stan Laurel and Oliver Hardy in the flesh, so to speak. The chap that took me to Bristol was a fan of motorcycle racing, so he decided that we should attend that evening's speedway meeting, and also see the brilliant comedy duo, who were to be special guests. As we walked towards the turnstiles, I was amazed at the crowds heading in the same direction. There certainly seemed to be many people pouring through the gates at Knowle Stadium and afterwards I learned that the attendance was some 12,000. I have often wondered since just how many were going for the same reason as me? I suspect not many!

The starting time drew near, there was the parade of officials and then there were attempts at various track records around the circuit, these featuring Billy Hole over one-lap, and Fred Tuck over two laps. Hole's effort was from a clutch start, while Tuck enjoyed the benefit of a flying start. The terms meant little or nothing to me at the time, but they certainly meant something to the gathered fans, since the lads on the track were loudly cheered. Then came event three, and this time four riders contested the race. There was a terrific noise as the four speedsters revved up their machines; and from the moment the tapes went up I was well and truly hooked! Jack Gordon of Wigan was the race winner from Bristol's Cyril Quick, and I simply couldn't wait for the next heat, and the next, and so on. The reason for my being there altered in a matter of seconds, and I don't think I could have cared less who was attending. All I was interested in was the black leather-clad boys serving up the thrills on the track! After that exciting evening I made up my mind to learn as much about Bristol Speedway as I could, as well as the sport in general. Knowle Stadium, it seemed, had been staging league racing since 1936, and although their nickname was the 'Bulldogs' (it really couldn't be anything else, could it?), back in the pre-war days they actually had a Dexter bull as their mascot (this is a small breed of cattle, just like a Shetland pony is to the horse world). The bull went by the name of Joey, and often visited the track to wish his charges luck. Oh yes, and another character was the Bristol team's own page boy – a lad decked out in a uniform and pill box hat, who went by the name of 'Sunshine'. Later on, I learned that the Supporters' Club, a very large and active organization, was run by a Miss Jean Pomphrey, who sent out Christmas cards to all the members.

I was fortunate to be able to attend many other meetings over the years at Knowle, and thoroughly enjoyed them all. If there was one track/club in speedway that was like a big, happy family, it was Bristol. This included the riders, many of whom signed on in 1946, and were still sporting the famous orange and black colours years later when falling attendances forced the club to close down. Such was the deep love everyone had for the side, that it was reported in the tough days of 1955, when things weren't going too well, that the riders offered to take a pay cut if it would help. Sadly, it didn't and the Bulldogs were forced to close in June of that year. Then, in 1960, there was the advent of the Provincial League, and having 'tested the water' with a series of open-licence meetings the year before, we saw league racing return to Knowle Stadium. Not only that, but there were a few names from the past, who donned leathers again, or came back home to help re-establish Bristol Bulldogs. It was marvellous, but unfortunately the stadium fell to the developers, and the fans had to wait until 1977 to hear the roar of the speedway again on a new circuit at Eastville Stadium. Although the attendances were amazing in speedway terms, Eastville was an acquired taste. Personally, I didn't care too much for the racing, but it did bring out new stars for the famous Bulldogs, especially Phil Crump, Phil Herne, Steve Gresham, and the female fans' 'heart-throb' Tormod Langli.

Sadly, Bristol has no track these days, but there is racing at Highbridge in Somerset. However, it really is a great pity that a city, which successfully staged the sport for so long, has no circuit of its own. Hopefully one day it will have, and then the story of the Bulldogs can be continued. In the meantime, I trust that a reminder of a few of the lads who made Bristol great in years gone by, will bring back a host of memories – and all of them happy.

By the way, Stan Laurel and Oliver Hardy did make an appearance on that July evening in 1947, but by then I had added to my list of heroes.

Glynn Shailes
July 2003

50 Bristol Bulldogs Greats

Ernie Baker	*Tormod Langli*
Mike Beddoe	Fred Leavis
Jack Bibby	Norman Lindsay
Nigel Boocock	Jeff Lloyd
Chris Boss	Bill Maddern
Dick Bradley	*Cordy Milne*
Bill Clibbett	Wal Morton
Eric Collins	*Jack Mountford*
Cliff Cox	Olle Nygren
George Craig	Tom Oakley
Bruce Cribb	*Geoff Pymar*
Phil Crump	Cyril Quick
Roy Dook	Trevor Redmond
Vic Duggan	Bill Rogers
Mike Erskine	*Eric Salmon*
Frank Evans	*Harry Shepherd*
Pat Flanagan	Bert Spencer
Steve Gresham	Rol Stobart
Morian Hansen	Nobby Stock
Phil Herne	Jack Summers
Billy Hole	Chum Taylor
Johnny Hole	Roy Taylor
Ron Howes	*Fred Tuck*
Henny Kroeze	*Jack Unstead*
Reg Lambourne	*Roger Wise*

The twenty who appear here in italics, occupy three pages instead of the usual two.

Competition	Matches	Points
League	17	98
Provincial League KOC	4	16
Western Cup	3	11
Challenge	4	29
4 Team Tournament	2	19
Bulldogs Total	**30**	**173**

Ernest Baker was born in London on 18 August 1931, and like so many riders before him, he began his career at Rye House. At the time (1956), the Hertfordshire outfit participated in the Southern Area League, and whilst this had only four teams, it nonetheless provided youngsters with the opportunity to gain valuable experience. Competition for team places was understandably keen, but at least Ernie managed to open his scoring account, recording 3 points as part of the squad that secured the league title. The following year, speedway was very much in the doldrums, with just eleven sides in the National League, plus four in the Southern Area League. Rye House underwent a change of ownership, and were unable to repeat their success of the previous season, actually slumping to the foot of the table. Ernie remained on board, but getting rides was difficult, and he ended the campaign with just 8 points to his name.

The 1958 season dawned, but there was no Rye House in the lower league for Ernie to continue his training and desire to make good in speedway. Instead, a new Junior League had been formed, comprising 'second' teams from National League outfits Norwich, Poole and Swindon, with open-licence venue Yarmouth taking the number of participants to four. However, the league was to end in disarray with the fixtures not completed. Ernie had joined Yarmouth, and they had certainly put a very useful side together, but they only raced in away matches at Norwich and Swindon, with their own supporters never seeing them in action on their home strip at Caister Road. Ernie represented the Norfolk team in their match at Swindon on 12 July, netting 1+1 points from two starts as the powerful visitors romped to a 40½-19½ victory. In the second-half of the programme, the Blunsdon raceway played host to the Junior Riders' Individual Championship, with Ernie showing great potential to record two second places and a third, on his way to a 5-point tally.

With the Southern Area League subsequently being reformed, the 1959 season was to prove a good one for him. Ernie returned to his first love Rye House, and riding with a greater degree of confidence, he plundered a total of 40 points to finish third in the club's scoring stakes. Meanwhile, he was also given opportunities at Wimbledon in the National Reserve League, and although a lot of fixtures were left outstanding, he still registered 13 points for the junior Dons.

The Provincial League was born in 1960, and Ernie went 'west' to link with Bristol for what was an extremely enjoyable campaign. He certainly made a mark in his debut for the Bulldogs, scoring 9 points in a challenge match at Cradley Heath on 23 April, after which he was a regular in the side. In the league, Ernie proved to be a particularly potent force at Knowle; the highlights of his year being brilliant paid maximums in successive matches against Edinburgh (11+1) on 27 May, and Liverpool (9+3) on the 3 June. He also knocked-up scores of 10 when both Bradford and Cradley Heath visited, while his best away performances occurred at Rayleigh (8) and Poole (7+1). Having ridden in 17 league matches, and totalled 98 points, it was no surprise that his figures were sufficient to place him fourth in the Bristol scoring behind the heat-leader trio of Trevor Redmond, Johnny Hole and Cliff Cox. There can be no doubt that Ernie provided much valued back-up to the top three, and this was a major factor as the Bulldogs very nearly took the title, only just finishing behind Rayleigh and Poole in the end. However, it was a different story in the Knock-Out Cup, as Bristol went all the way to lift the trophy, thanks to a 100-89 aggregate victory over Rayleigh in the final. Happily, Ernie was a member of the Bulldogs septet throughout the glory run, with his highest score being 9 points in the first round at Bradford on 25 June. When Bristol were forced to close after such a good year, Ernie accompanied much of the side to ride for Plymouth in 1961.

Unfortunately, he couldn't come to terms with the Pennycross circuit, and moved on to pastures new with Wolverhampton, for whom he had notched 34 league points, prior to suffering spinal injuries in June, which kept him out of action for the remainder of the season.

Returning to the saddle in 1962, he revealed his best form to accumulate 132 points for Wolverhampton, only finishing behind Graham Warren and Tommy Sweetman in the club's end-of-year statistics. He also had limited outings with Wimbledon in the National League, but obviously the going was tough and he only managed to record 11 points.

In 1963, whilst again representing Wolverhampton, Ernie was involved in a high-speed crash at Edinburgh, which left him nursing a dislocated shoulder, and restricted his season's scoring to just 57 points for the Midlanders, plus just 3 for Wimbledon.

Ernie rode solely for the Dons in 1964, but with limited chances, he could only muster 11 points, and then seemed lost to the sport. He did, however, return in 1966 with Hackney, riding in 32 matches for 71 points, and a league average of 3.37. He then seemed to drift away from the scene, before being tempted back by injury-hit Wolverhampton late in 1967, when he scored 6 points in 4 league fixtures. After missing the whole of 1968, Ernie once more donned his racing gear for one final fling with Ipswich in 1969. It proved a great swansong too, as he raced to 146 points in 26 matches for a league average of 6.41, and supplied solid middle-order strength to the Witches line-up. However, it is at Bristol that one has fond memories of Ernie Baker, who as a rider always gave his best in backing the Bulldogs top-end with several outstanding performances, and plenty of handy returns.

Competition	Matches	Points
League	126	641½
National Trophy	12	52
British Speedway Cup	9	61
Anniversary Cup	3	22
Spring Cup	6	30
Challenge	37	166
Mini-Matches	3	13
Bulldogs Total	**196**	**985½**

Michael Beddoe was born in Bolton, Greater Manchester on 23 May 1923. He had been a scrambles and trials rider before he decided to purchase an old Rudge machine in order to give grass-track racing a go in 1946. This proved to be another step on the road that eventually led to him having a go on the cinders.

Having moved down to live in Bristol, locally-born New Cross teamster Les Wotton loaned him a speedway machine and Mike had a series of trials at Knowle Stadium. This was at a time when Bristol were running open-licence meetings with a view to applying for league status the following year. Mike so impressed the Bulldogs management that he gained a place in the side's first challenge match against Birmingham on 2 August, when he notched a tally of 2+1 points. At the end of their short run of fixtures, he had represented the club on eight occasions and done enough to claim a team place in 1947. Bristol duly finished their Second Division campaign in sixth position out of the eight sides, with Mike sensationally topping the scoring on 199½ points.

He remained on board the following season and was again piling up the points, when the Bulldogs visited Fleetwood for a league encounter on 11 May. The match was close

throughout and everything rested on the last heat, when Mike and team-mate Roger Wise faced the Fleetwood duo of Jack Gordon and Cyril Cooper. The exciting race that followed is best described in an article penned by Mike Craven in *The Speedway Researcher*: 'On the final bend, Wise was in the lead, Gordon second and Cooper third, with Beddoe trailing in last place. A magnificent final spurt by Beddoe saw him pass Cooper and almost squeeze past Gordon on the line. However, for one reason or another, Beddoe was too close to the fence and crashed with disastrous consequences. His third place had already given Bristol the match by a single point (42-41), but ensuing mayhem and heated argument in the pits over the cause of the accident marred a wonderful evening's entertainment by both sides.' Poor Mike had careered into the corrugated safety fence, suffering a serious foot injury. Sadly, it was diagnosed that part of his right foot had to be amputated, and the operation took place at the Blackpool Victoria Hospital the following day. This was a terrible shame as he had accumulated 77 points from 11 matches at that stage, and would have contributed a lot more as the Bulldogs swept all before them to win the League Championship.

Although he always stated that he wanted to ride again, it was to the total amazement of everyone, when he actually did make a comeback in 1949. Clearly, he was never going to be the same rider again, but it was still some return as he played a full part, scoring 232 points as the Bulldogs again won the Second Division Championship.

In 1950, Bristol were successful in their application to be promoted to Division One, but having received no help with rider allocations to strengthen their squad, they had to rely on the men who had served them so well at the lower level. So here was Mike Beddoe, still working hard to boost his confidence after a serious foot injury, thrust into the lions den of First Division racing! He was mainly used at reserve and although the going was particularly hard, he still plugged away to accumulate a respectable total of 72 points as the Bulldogs finished seventh out of nine teams. Mike's tally was garnered from 20 league matches and his season could rightly be described as eventful. On 16 May, he tumbled at West Ham, but despite having two heavy plaster patches on his face, he still lined up in the very next match.

Unfortunately, his season was subsequently curtailed when he suffered a broken knee while representing Bristol in a challenge match at Shelbourne on 23 July.

He might have been diminutive in stature, but Mike was as courageous as they come and he once again donned a Bulldogs race-jacket at the start of the 1951 campaign. The racing seemed to be getting harder at that level, and he was to lose his team place after failing to score from two starts at New Cross on 22 August. At the time, he had struggled to attain 57 points from 23 league matches, but that wasn't the end of his racing career as he then linked up with ex-Bristol promoter Reg Witcomb at Third Division Swindon. The Robins' boss had been on the look out for someone after Ray Ellis had suffered a fractured skull in a bad track spill at Exeter on 20 August. Having joined on loan, Mike duly made his Swindon debut in a home match against Rayleigh on 8 September, when he netted 2+1 points from two starts. He went on to total nine league appearances for the Robins, his best performances being scores of 8+1 at Long Eaton, and 7 at Aldershot. His mini-stint yielded a total of 32 points for an average of 5.33, and he also appeared in a Blunsdon-staged challenge match against Bristol on 13 October, when his former team-mates ran riot to win 57-27.

Mike was back at Bristol in 1952, but having ridden in just four league matches for the club, he linked with Wimbledon in July and subsequently retired at the end of the campaign.

To end, there is a delightful little tale concerning Mike, told by a former team-mate. It happened long after Knowle Stadium had closed down, and a housing estate had been built on the spot where for many years Bristol fans had stood to cheer on their heroes. Mike, it appears, had to deliver a parcel to a house standing where the old starting gate had stood. Having handed the package to the lady of the house, and whilst stood in her kitchen, Mike remarked 'Madam, I made some wonderful starts from where your cooker now stands!' What's more, he probably did too!

Competition	Matches	Points
League	14	70½
National Trophy	4	27
Provincial Trophy	1	8
English Speedway Trophy	6	29
Union Cup	2	10
Challenge	2	9
Bulldogs Total	**29**	**153½**

Jack Bibby was born on 24 September 1910, in Harrietville, Victoria, Australia, and first came to this country to race when the great Vic Huxley brought him over in 1934. Prior to that, it appears he began his racing career in his native land almost by accident when a pal entered him for a race which he promptly went and won!

Upon arriving on these shores, he was signed up by Lea Bridge, later that year moving to Walthamstow when the Leyton operation was closed by the Control Board due to what were described as 'continuing irregularities'. After missing a year of British racing, Jack returned in 1936, having agreed to race for Cardiff in the Provincial League. However, he was to miss the start of the

season at the White City Stadium, since he was still on the boat travelling over from his Aussie homeland, and due to his late arrival, he ended up at Plymouth instead. Although the Devon side didn't have a very good time of it, actually finishing bottom of the league, Jack proved to be one of their more productive riders, scoring 74 points from 14 matches.

After an absence of two seasons, he again journeyed back over to the UK in 1939, when he linked with Bristol, who at the time, were operating in Division Two of the National League. His stint with the Bulldogs couldn't possibly have started any better, as he registered a full 12-point maximum on his club debut in an English Speedway Trophy encounter away at Crystal Palace on 22 April, helping his new side to a 46-33 success. Programmed at reserve, he was a tad fortunate to remain unbeaten, for in heat thirteen he developed mechanical problems while heading the race, thus giving home man Mick Mitchell the lead. However, on the third lap, the Palace man shed a chain, leaving Jack to coast home first in a time of 92.6 seconds – some 11 seconds outside Tiger Stevenson's track record for the Sydenham circuit!

Although he never again scaled such dizzy heights for the Bulldogs, Jack obviously had a liking for the 449-yard London raceway. On Bristol's return for a National Trophy tie on

27 May, he hit 10+1 points in an even bigger 65-35 victory. That, incidentally was one of two matches the Bulldogs raced in London that day, as they later lost 53-29 in a league fixture at Hackney Wick, with Jack netting but a single point, plus a bonus. Ironically, four days prior to that, he had knocked-up what turned out to be his highest score for Bristol in league racing, against Hackney Wick in a 48-35 win at Knowle, with only Bill Clibbett's four-ride full-house bettering his tally of 9+1 points in the home camp.

Whilst Jack was a useful team member, he tended to suffer from inconsistency. On his day, he was equal to anyone around the Knowle circuit, yet there were times when he struggled. One match that he especially enjoyed occurred on 23 June, when Norwich visited the West Country for a league fixture. Led by another 12-point maximum from Bill Clibbett, Bristol ran riot to claim a 63-18 success, with Jack gleaning $8\frac{1}{2}$ points, plus 2 bonus. The half-point came about in the final heat, when Jack and team-mate Jeff Lloyd diced with each other for the duration, and couldn't be separated as they crossed the line in a blur, both subsequently being awarded $2\frac{1}{2}$ points.

Sadly, at the end of August, racing was suspended due to the outbreak of the Second World War, and at the time, Jack had appeared in all 14 league matches ridden by the Bulldogs, scoring a total of $70\frac{1}{2}$ points in the process. The Australian was to be based in London throughout the hostilities, where he played an important role serving in the National Fire Service.

With the war over, he resumed racing in the newly-formed Northern League, and settled down well to garner $109\frac{1}{2}$ league points for Sheffield, helping the South Yorkshire side to occupy second position in the final table. Bristol had also reopened that year, running a series of open-licence meetings at Knowle Stadium, and Jack was more than happy to

don a Bulldogs race-jacket again on 9 August, when he scored 5 points in a thrilling 41-41 draw against Newcastle.

Remaining with Sheffield, he did even better in 1947, ending up as second-highest scorer behind Tommy Bateman on 219 points as the Tigers again finished as runners-up, this time in Division Two of the National League. Jack was to stay with Sheffield throughout 1948 and 1949, during which time he continued to serve the Tigers well, recording league tallies of 129 and 172 points respectively.

Having returned to his native land for the winter, among other meetings, Jack made one appearance in the 1949/50 Test series against England at Marlbyrnong Speedway in Melbourne on 11 February, when the tourists gained a 58-50 success. Unfortunately, having scored 3 points, Jack was involved in a heat seventeen crash which left him suffering a fractured left thigh, causing him to miss the entire British season.

A return to the saddle in 1951 saw him ride in a match for Ashfield (Glasgow) prior to dropping down a division to assist Cardiff, who were having a tough time with injuries to key riders. It was strange to think that he almost represented the Welsh side many moons before at their previous White City Stadium home in 1936, and here he was finally racing for Cardiff some fifteen years later at a different venue in Penarth Road! His appearances for the Dragons were limited, and having netted 17 league points, he disappeared from the speedway scene.

Despite only spending a curtailed year with Bristol, Jack is fondly remembered by old-time fans of the men in orange and black. When he represented the Dominions in a Test match against England at Knowle Stadium on 14 July 1939, he was aptly described in the programme as 'a modest, quiet sort of fellow, who gets on with his job', and Jack, you may be sure, would have approved of those sentiments.

Competition	Matches	Points
League	68	369
Knock-Out Cup	6	31
Inter League KOC	4	17
Spring Gold Cup	6	32
Challenge	11	37
4 Team Tournament	9	40
Bulldogs Total	**104**	**526**

Nigel Boocock was born in Wakefield, Yorkshire on 17 September 1937, and was most certainly one of the greatest riders to ever pull on an England breastplate.

He joined Bristol in 1977, towards the end of his outstanding riding career, following many years as the Coventry number one. Charles Ochiltree, the promoter at the Warwickshire venue, was rebuilding his side for the future, and as an essential part of that exercise, had signed Danish ace Ole Olsen in 1976. At the end of that season, Nigel said 'goodbye' to the Bees after no less than eighteen years with the club. He had retired and emigrated to Sydney, Australia, but Bristol boss Wally Mawdsley tempted him back to join his new set-up at Eastville Stadium. The shrewd promoter knew that in signing 'Booey' for his team, he was getting a rider who always gave 100 per cent in his racing, and could ride on any circuit. His best racing days were perhaps behind him, but his experience and speedway know-how was

second to none, and would obviously greatly help in the re-establishment of the sport in the City, which had last been staged at Knowle Stadium in 1960.

Nigel's career had begun way back in 1954, when he had a few second-half spins at Belle Vue. The following season he broke into the Odsal team that was competing in Division One of the old National League. Although he only totalled 12 league points in his first year, he impressed the supporters of the Tudors by always trying his heart out for the whole four laps of every single race. He may have lacked experience and was a bit raw, but he just never gave up. In 1956, Nigel was quick to show the Odsal management how much he had learned, finishing second in the side's league scoring behind the great Arthur Forrest, with a most creditable tally of 135 points.

By 1957, the future of speedway looked bleak, and with Bradford (as Odsal had been re-titled) only running open-licence meetings, Nigel was posted to Birmingham, where his all-out style earned him many new fans. Unfortunately, the West Midlanders withdrew from the league in mid-season, but Bradford were ready and willing to step back in and take over their remaining fixtures, so Nigel found himself returning to his old home base. Despite the disruption, he enjoyed another good year, his tally of 175 league points being made up of 78 for the Brummies, and 97 for the Tudors. With Bradford closing down at the end of the season, Nigel moved on to Ipswich in 1958, and although the Witches had a torrid time of it, finishing last in the league, he still managed to record 104 valuable points.

So to 1959, when the Yorkshireman began his long love affair with the Coventry management and supporters. He had previously ridden for Great Britain on one occasion in Sweden in 1956, and also participated in one meeting for England versus Poland in 1958, but once he became a Bee, the international honours just flooded in. Meanwhile, on the individual front, after two non-riding appearances as reserve, the first while with Odsal in 1956, 'Booey' went on to ride in the World Final on eight occasions, his best performance being 10 points at Wembley Stadium in 1969. In the British Final, he made a total of 13 appearances, and although he was never crowned Champion, he finished as runner-up no less than three times in 1965, 1969 and 1972.

In what was a glittering career, he was also present for the prestigious British League Riders' Championship on eight occasions, with his best showing being a second place behind the one and only Barry Briggs in 1967. Known as 'Little Boy Blue' on account of his blue leathers, Nigel enjoyed a phenomenal career with Coventry, scoring a total of 1,034 league points for the club in the pre-British League era from 1959-1964. Then, in the first season of the new league (1965), he remained ever-present throughout the 34-match programme to notch 381 points for a huge average of 11.09, which was sufficient for him to occupy pole position in the entire league.

Nigel continued to score heavily for the Bees over the years, accumulating an amazing total of 4,028 points from 390 league matches between 1965-1976 inclusive. That gave him a club total of 5,062 points in league matches alone, not to mention all the various cup competitions and challenge matches etc.

It must have been strange to line-up for another team after so long with one club, but

he was to make his debut for Bristol on 24 June 1977, when he netted 6+2 points in a 59-19 league success, ironically against Coventry! As the season progressed, he adapted to the strange sand-covered Eastville circuit, and there were several double-figure returns, including a paid maximum (11+1) against Ipswich, and scores of 10+1, 12+1, and 10+2 against Hull, Hackney Wick, and Belle Vue respectively. He wasn't quite so effective on the Bulldogs travels, but even so, he was still a useful man to have around and he ended the campaign with a total of 192 points from 32 league matches for an average of 6.33. 'Booey' obviously enjoyed the 'Eastville Experience', what with the huge crowds that regularly poured through the turnstiles and the terrific atmosphere that was generated. Lining up for the Bulldogs again in 1978, he was generally good for half-a-dozen points, with the high spots of his year being tallies of 9+3 against Sheffield, and 9+1 against Cradley Heath in home matches and, whilst on the road, he netted scores of 9, 8+3 and 8+1 at Halifax, Wimbledon and Coventry respectively.

He was to be the only ever-present rider in the camp, but although he always gave everything in his races, time was catching up with him, as emphasized by his end of term average of 5.77, having recorded 177 points from Bristol's 36 league matches. Nigel did make the odd appearance at British League level during what turned out to be his last couple of years in the saddle, representing both Exeter (1979) and Swindon (1980). However, he primarily rode in the National League, firstly with Canterbury in 1979, when he recorded 279 league points, and then for Exeter in 1980, when the Devonians dropped down from the top-flight, finishing with a haul of 324 points.

Retirement soon beckoned and he returned to Australia, this time for good. He will always be regarded as one of this country's most brilliant riders, and a man who just never gave up when out on the track.

Competition	Matches	Points
League	135	583
National Trophy	17	68
Spring Cup	6	24
Coronation Cup	16	69
Southern Shield	7	31
Challenge	54	230
4 Team Tournment	2	11
Mini Matches	4	6
Junior League	37	137
Bulldogs Total	**278**	**1,159**

Christopher Boss was born in Barry, South Glamorgan on 12 June 1925, and throughout his career in speedway he rode entirely for Bristol. Prior to becoming a Bulldog in 1949, he had competed in grass-track events and with some success too.

The story goes that after Chris had taken his early rides at Knowle Stadium, the Bristol manager Bill Hamblin described him as 'a natural speedway rider', and as things turned out this comment proved to be spot on. He was to learn the rudiments of the sport quickly in the second-half events around the Knowle circuit, prior to making his Bulldogs debut in an away league fixture at Walthamstow on 1 August. Unfortunately, it was something of an inauspicious start for the Welsh youngster, as not only did he fail to score, but Bristol also suffered a 46-37 defeat. However, the following evening the Bulldogs were in further league action at Southampton and in a tight affair, it was the men in orange and black who dug deep to secure a 42-41 success. Chris came up trumps with 4 points, his contribution playing a valuable part in the victory, especially when he grabbed a vital second place in the penultimate heat.

Remembering that there were no guests or rider replacement facilities in those days, Chris was mainly to be used in the side as cover for injuries, but he did manage to make 13 league appearances, netting a total of 26 points. His wholehearted performances had certainly pleased the Bristol public, although a number of folk did express concern about the number of mechanical problems he suffered. Speedway has always been an expensive sport, and as Chris only had one machine, he had no back-up when it failed him. Therefore, the generous Knowle regulars organized a collection to allow him to purchase a new bike, raising a total of £100, which was a substantial sum at the time.

As the history books tell us, Bristol were promoted to Division One in 1950, and Chris decided to stay on board and fight for a team place. Aside from the usual second-half scratch events, he was to be a regular in the Junior League side, but with the matches decided over just two heats, it meant there was not a lot of racing for a young man anxious for rides. In the event, he was to remain ever-present throughout the Junior League campaign, recording 114 points from 32 matches as he helped his side to the claim the Championship ahead of New Cross and Wembley. Chris did get several opportunities in the main Bristol side as well, making 14 league appearances, and with 50 points to his name he was seen to be continuing to improve rapidly. His best performance of the season occurred in a home league fixture with Wimbledon on 29 September, when he raced to 8+2 points as the Bulldogs took victory by 50-33 scoreline.

Chris came on in leaps and bounds in 1951, racing in all but one of the matches in the Bulldogs 32-match league programme, while more importantly, netting an impressive tally of 141 points. On 14 September, he covered himself in glory by scoring 10+1 points against a West Ham side that included Aub Lawson, Arthur Atkinson and Malcolm Craven; his wonderful display paving the way for Bristol to narrowly win the league encounter 44-40. A month later, on 13 October, the Bulldogs travelled the short distance to appear at the Blunsdon home of Division Three side Swindon in a challenge match. The meeting brought Bristol face to face with their former promoter Reg Witcomb, but following the pre-match pleasantries, the men from Knowle simply let rip to win easily by 57 points to 27. Chris was undoubtedly the man of the match, having romped to an inspired four-ride maximum.

Bristol, 1949. From left to right: Roger Wise, Mike Beddoe, Dick Bradley, Jack Mountford, Bill Hamblin (Team manager), Billy Hole, Chris Boss and Graham Hole.

So to 1952, and it was another year of progress as the Welshman remained everpresent in the Bulldogs 36 league matches, and jumped into second place in the side's scoring with 225 points. He put together an increased number of double-figure returns, with his best effort being a 12-point maximum in a league match against Norwich at Knowle on 1 August, when the West Country boys ran riot to win 64-20. Chris wasn't such a force on the away circuits, although there were several fine showings, not least of which was a 10-point return at Odsal on 13 September.

The 1953 season came along, with great things expected from Chris, but sadly it wasn't to be. The league programme was scaled down to just 16 matches, and he was to miss just one, when the Bulldogs visited West Ham. His scoring went on a downward slide, and he totalled just 70 points, with the 1954 Stenners Annual describing him as 'Always threatening, never quite getting there.' There was the odd flash of brilliance, especially on 17 July, when he registered a paid maximum (10+2 points) against West Ham in a league match at Knowle. He also raced to 11 points when Bristol entertained Birmingham on 4 September; but these were to be the only two occasions he struck double-figures during the league campaign. Chris did, however, reveal his best form in another challenge match at Swindon on 5 September, when he was credited with a 12-point maximum, as the Bulldogs had little difficulty in gaining a 53-28 victory.

Looking at 1954, it is sad to relate that rather than regaining his golden touch, by and large his form continued to wane, and this was a year when the Bulldogs chose to race in Division Two. Just 52 points from 19 league matches was scant reward for a rider, who just two years previously, had looked to be on the way to becoming a world beater. He became rather patchy to say the least, sometimes there were flashes of the Chris Boss of old, but these tended to be few and far between. It was an excellent season as far as the club was concerned, with the Bulldogs winning the League Championship ahead of Poole, but for the man from Barry, it was not a good year to remember. It is well documented that Bristol were forced to close down in June 1955, due to poor attendance figures. Chris endured another lean time of it, recording just 19 points from 7 league matches, and when the Bulldogs shut their doors, it was no surprise when he called it a day and hung up his leathers. He did, however, make a fleeting return for the club in 1959, appearing in a couple of meetings as the roar of the bikes resumed at Knowle Stadium in a series of open-licence events.

Having ridden only for Bristol, he had been a loyal club servant, rising close to the top in Division One, before, disappointingly, coming back down almost as fast. However, he should be remembered for his 1952 season, when he proved he could beat the best that Division One had to offer.

Competition	Matches	Points
League	195	1,345
National Trophy	28	283
Anniversary Cup	1	7
Coronation Cup	16	142
Southern Shield	12	119
Spring Cup	6	46
Challenge	68	$593\frac{1}{2}$
4 Team Tournament	3	24
3 Team Tournament	1	9
Mini-Matches	7	34
Junior League	1	2
Bulldogs Total	**338**	**$2,604\frac{1}{2}$**

Derrick Edwin Bradley was born on 28 November 1924, in Netheravon, Wiltshire, but throughout the world of speedway and grass-track racing, he was always known simply as Dick.

He began racing on the grass circuits at around the same time as his future Bristol team-mate Mike Beddoe, and he became a protégé of another post-war Bulldogs favourite, Roger Wise. The progression to speedway seemed a natural one, and Dick was signed by Bristol for the 1948 season, starting his shale-shifting career in the second-half events at Knowle Stadium. His progress was initially slow but sure, with his big break coming when Jack Mountford had a dose of 'flu, and Dick was called up to make his club debut in a league match at Fleetwood on 14 September, when he understandably failed to trouble the scorers. That was the first of only three league matches he appeared in that year and his lack of experience was emphasized by the fact that he

managed to glean a total of just 3 points from them. However, he did produce one outstanding performance, revealing tremendous potential, when he raced to 7+2 points from three starts in an Anniversary Cup match against Norwich at Knowle on 22 October.

The Bristol management clearly had a lot of faith in Dick, for he was given a team berth right from the start of the 1949 season. He continued to progress well too, remaining ever-present throughout the 44-match league programme to net 129 points, as the Bulldogs retained the Division Two Championship they had claimed a year previously. Late in the season, Dick particularly enjoyed a home match against Norwich on 14 October, when he raced to a wonderful paid maximum (9+3 points). The meeting resulted in a huge 68-16 success for Bristol, as they very nearly repeated the maximum possible result they had achieved the week before, when crushing Glasgow 70-14. That represented Dick's best home performance in the league, clearly paving the way for a greater success in 1950. However, with the Bulldogs back-to-back Division Two title successes, they were finally promoted to the top-flight, and although Dick had developed as a rider, he had serious doubts about his ability to cope with racing in what was the toughest speedway league in the world. Swindon, his local track had opened in 1949, and Dick thought he might be more at home riding under his former boss Reg Witcomb in the less demanding echelons of Division Three racing. Happily for both the rider himself, and the Bristol management, Dick was to remain with the Bulldogs, and despite his reservations, he was to take the cut and thrust of Division One racing in his stride. Completing a full season of 32 league matches, he became one of the best riders in the Bristol camp, accumulating a magnificent 184 points, and finishing second only to skipper Billy Hole in the scoring stakes. The highlight of his year undoubtedly occurred when Bristol made their second visit of the campaign to Harringay on 8 September. That was when the Bulldogs rode out of their skins to record their only away league victory of the year by 47 points to 37, with Dick's contribution being a quite magnificent 12-point maximum.

So to 1951, and having proved he could 'mix it' with the best, Dick was to go on to even greater things, plundering 264 league points as he again remained ever-present over the 32-match programme. So well did he go in fact, that only newest Bulldog Geoff Pymar scored more points (Geoff had joined in June the previous season). 'Bradley was out-standing' was the comment made by eminent speedway journalist and photographer Peter Morrish. Dick showed his class by qualifying for the Wembley-staged World Final as reserve, and he actually got to ride in heat eighteen when he replaced Ernie Roccio. The race itself saw him engage in a tremendous track battle with Alan Hunt for second place, and he eventually got the better of the duel to finish behind the victorius Louis Lawson, thereby showing he was as good as any rider in Division One.

In 1952, Dick put together another terrific season, and although Bristol finished near the bottom of the table, he was their shining light, particularly on the away tracks. The end-of-year statistics gave him a total of 255 points from 35 league meetings, and for the first time he headed the club's scoring. Along the way, he registered 3 maximums at Knowle against Birmingham (12), Harringay (10+2) and Norwich (9+3). Individually, he again made

it through to the World Final and began in brilliant fashion with 8 points from his first three outings. He was only able to manage a single point from his other two rides, which was a shame since his earlier heats had suggested he might well have claimed a rostrum position. On 12 September, six days before the Wembley showdown, Dick had made his Test-match debut for England against Australia at Harringay and his performance was to set the speedway world alight. Due to injuries, he was drafted into the team at the last minute, and wasn't even programmed. It is fair to say he wasn't particularly keen on making the trip to Harringay because as second reserve, he was unlikely to get a ride. Also, with the meeting being staged on a Friday, it meant missing Bristol's home match against Odsal, thereby breaking his ever-present sequence that stretched back to the start of 1949. As things turned out, Dick's performance was real 'Roy of the Rovers' stuff, as he powered his way to a 16-point haul from six starts, and inspired England to a narrow 55-53 success.

By 1953, Dick was established as one of the best riders in the country. With 119 points from the shortened 16-match league campaign, he headed the Bulldogs scorechart – in many fixtures it was a case of Dick Bradley versus the opposition, and it was little surprise that the side slumped to the foot of the Division One table. Dick again reached the World Final, but after a good second place in his first ride, he unfortunately lost his touch and didn't score again. Sadly, that was to be the last time he graced speedway's premier meeting. In 1954, Bristol applied for, and were granted a place in Division Two, where the operational costs would be less. Having been 'demoted', they promptly charged to the League Champion-ship, finishing 4 points ahead of a powerful Poole outfit. Dick, as expected, topped the team's scoring with 188 league points from 19 matches, and was naturally one of the best riders in the entire division, only being out-scored by Leicester's Ken McKinlay in fact.

Disappointingly, the crowd figures had dwindled at Bristol, and even the brilliance of Dick could not entice them through the

turnstiles. In 1955, things were no better, and to try and help the situation, the riders even offered to take a temporary pay cut. The management wouldn't accept this gesture though, and the club subsequently resigned from the league in June, after completing just 14 matches.

Having appeared in every match, Dick was way out on top of the scoring with a huge tally of 203 points. Although he could have easily then returned to top-flight racing, Dick opted to join Charlie Knott and his Division Two set-up at Southampton, making his debut for the side against Poole in a National Trophy match at Banister Court on 21 June. It was a move he never regretted, and he was to remain with the Saints until they closed down at the end of the 1963 season, during which time he plundered a total of 1,343 league points to become the second highest scorer in club's history, behind Jimmy Squibb. During his time with the Hampshire outfit, Dick again donned a Bulldogs bib on five occasions in 1959 (scoring 48 points), when the sport

returned to Knowle Stadium for a short run of open-licence meetings.

A move into the Provincial League with Newport followed in 1964, when there was no let up in the scoring as he amassed 170 league points. With the formation of the British League, Dick again lined up for the Wasps in 1965, but after breaking an arm in a track accident, he decided to call it a day. This was a great pity, as he had ridden in 20 league matches for an average of 8.05, and there appeared to be plenty more to come.

It was following the retirement of Norman Parker that Dick then arrived to take charge as team manager of Swindon in 1968, and he stayed in place, doing much fine work, until the speedway promotion was taken over by Wally Mawdsley at the end of 1978.

Dick Bradley was without doubt one of the finest riders to race for Bristol, and it is likely that his loyalty to the club cost him many honours, since the Bulldogs were always regarded as 'unfashionable' in the old Division One set-up.

Competition	Matches	Points
League	32	190
National Trophy	5	34
Provincial Trophy	1	4
ACU Cup	6	$37\frac{1}{2}$
Union Cup	2	13
Challenge	8	$42\frac{1}{2}$
Bulldogs Total	**54**	**321**

William Clibbett was a Bristol-born rider who joined his hometown team after the 1938 season had got underway, having had a rethink about retiring.

He was a man of considerable experience when he arrived at Knowle, having begun his career on cinders at Portsmouth in 1930, when open-licence events were staged at the Wessex Stadium. That same year saw him represent Harringay in the Southern League and he was to again line-up for the London club in 1931, before later moving on to Wimbledon. A further change of scenery saw Bill travel to the West Country in 1932, when he linked with Plymouth, and he was to go on and complete three seasons of National League activity with the Devon outfit. While with them, he reached the Star Champ-ionship final in 1932, when he was eliminated after only running a third in his heat, and he also enjoyed a particularly good domestic campaign in 1933, when he appeared in 31

league fixtures, scoring 155 points for a very healthy 7.05 average.

In 1935, Bill joined Hackney Wick, who were embarking on their first season in the sport, and after settling quickly he went on to net 106 league points, providing great support to skipper Dicky Case, and fellow team-mates Dusty Haigh and Wally Lloyd. A major acquisition to the Hackney Wick team in 1936, saw the arrival of a rider, who, a couple of years later, would move with Bill to Bristol and skipper the Bulldogs – he was an American, and his name was Cordy Milne. Sadly, a tragic accident occurred at the London venue on 15 May, when the Wolves (as they were then known) faced West Ham in the ACU Cup. As could be expected in a derby match, there was some outstanding racing, with no quarter asked or given. There was cut and thrust racing throughout, and in heat fifteen, Bill lined-up along with partner Dusty Haigh, while the Hammers were represented by Tommy Croombs and Ken Brett. It was Dusty Haigh who made the gate, only to over-slide and fall on the first turn. Both of the West Ham boys tried to avoid the stricken rider, but he was unfortunately hit by one of the machines and died instantaneously to the great sadness of everyone in speedway at the time. Bill, who had fortunately missed the fallen riders and their bikes, just couldn't believe what had happened to his great friend, and although he continued on with his career in the sport, there were feelings amongst those who knew him that he was never quite the same after the shocking events of that May evening at Waterden Road. At the end of a difficult season, understandably his scoring in the league had dipped to 74 points, and he had slipped down to fifth place in the team's scoring.

He did, however, again sport the colours of the Wolves in 1938, when he mustered a tally of 68 league points, and later contemplated retirement. Attendances had fallen at Hackney Wick, and in 1938, the management sought permission to race on Saturday evenings in order to address the slide. This was subsequently refused by the Control Board, following an objection from Harringay, whose regular racenight was a Saturday. As a result, Hackney Wick applied for, and were granted authorization to race in the newly-formed Division Two, which had replaced the Provincial League. Bristol were promoted in their place, and the big three Wolves riders, Cordy Milne, Morian Hansen and Vic Duggan, were quickly fixed up with the Bulldogs, closely followed by a fourth in Bill. There had been some doubt about him joining Bristol, as was summed up by promoter Ronnie Greene in his programme notes: 'There is a big likelihood that he may retire from racing altogether. However, if he does ride, it will be for Bristol.' All of the ex-Hackney Wick men missed the opening meeting of the year at Knowle, an individual event, but with Bill happily on board, they took their places for a challenge match against New Cross, a week later on 15 April. Despite 13 points from Morian Hansen, and a dozen from Cordy Milne, the Bulldogs suffered a 62-43 reverse, with Bill's contribution being 3+1 points. Another four days passed before the North Americans visited in another challenge fixture, with Bristol faring much better, winning 43-41, and for Bill it was a good night since he recorded 8 points. Another highlight occurred on 3 June, when the Bulldogs entertained Belle Vue in the ACU Cup, and let rip for a 74-34 success, with a home man crossing the line first in all but two of the sixteen heats.

Bill and his skipper Cordy Milne couldn't be separated by the ACU Steward when they crossed the line in unison in heat thirteen, leaving the American with a match score of $17\frac{1}{2}$ points, and Bill with $10\frac{1}{2}$ points, plus 1 bonus. In Division One matches, Bill proved a steady gatherer of points, his best tallies at home being 8 against Wimbledon on 13 May, and 9 versus Belle Vue on 19 August.

Meanwhile, on team's travels, the high spots were somewhat strangely also gleaned against the same two opponents, with 9 points scored at Belle Vue on 7 May, and 8 at Wimbledon on 26 September. It all added up to a season's total of 117 points from 22 league matches, and fourth position in the Bristol scoring, behind former Hackney Wick colleagues Cordy Milne, Vic Duggan and Morian Hansen. It had been a disastrous year for the team as a whole, and with only six wins, plus a draw from their 24 Division One matches, they finished last in the table. It therefore came as little surprise when they

dropped down a league in 1939. That meant their top three stars moved on, and after initially deciding to retire, Bill opted to give the sport one more shot with the Bulldogs.

He marked his first match of the season in emphatic fashion too, scorching to a 15-point full-house in a huge 83-22 victory over Crystal Palace in a National Trophy tie at Knowle on 16 May. Although not quite hitting those heights again, his decision to return proved wise, for despite losing out on a few meetings through injury, he ended the curtailed campaign with 73 points from 10 league fixtures. Included in those figures were 12-point maximums in home matches against former club Hackney Wick on 23 May and Norwich on 23 June. One other performance really stood out against Norwich, when the Norfolk side visited Knowle for a Union Cup encounter on 18 August, with Bill netting 11 points as the Bulldogs collected a 44-39 win. Prior to that, a particularly proud moment occurred on 14 July, when he was chosen for England in the third Test match against the Dominions at Knowle. Although still recovering from a shin injury at the time, Bill managed to score $6\frac{1}{2}$ points for the host nation as they suffered a 63-44 reverse. He provided some thrills in heat seventeen too, when, in a dash to the line for third place, the ACU Steward could not split him and Dominions representative Ernie Evans, resulting in what was actually the second dead-heat of the evening! Doubtless, his end-of-term figures would have been even better had the Second World War not brought proceedings to an abrupt halt, and with it, his career. Nevertheless, Bill enjoyed the best part of two seasons with Bristol, and it pleased him to be known as the local boy made good.

Competition	Matches	Points
League	15	126
Provincial Trophy	7	65
Challenge	11	101
Bulldogs Total	**33**	**292**

Eric Collins hailed from the state of Queensland, Australia, and when he linked with Bristol in 1936, he was brought in as a rider who could lead from the front, with the ability to take on, and beat the best that the Provincial League had to offer.

His career in the UK initially began with Harringay in 1931, a season which later saw him represent Lea Bridge. In 1932, he raced for Plymouth, and in a fine year, he qualified for the Star Championship final, although injury sadly forced him to miss the big event. After two years off the British scene, he returned with Wimbledon in 1935, and it was as a Dons rider that he 'doubled-up' with Bristol the following season, the decision having been made that the West Country side, in their first season of league racing, would primarily serve as an excellent 'nursery' for the Londoners assets.

The opening meeting for Bristol duly took place at Nottingham on 28 April, and the newly-formed club enjoyed the best possible start to league racing when they secured a narrow 34-33 victory. With just 2+1 points, Eric might have made a quiet debut, but in view of the final score, this was indeed a vital contribution. It didn't take the Australian long to show the Bristol supporters what he could really do, however, as in the new team's first home match on 8 May, a league encounter against Southampton, he played a full part in a 38-32 success by storming to a four-ride maximum. Not only that, but he also returned the fastest time of the evening, and in clocking 74.0 seconds, he established the track record for the 290-yard circuit, which, when previously used for the initial handicap and scratch style races between 1928-30, had been measured at 344 yards. Following a 6+1 return against Cardiff a week later, the Bristol boys journeyed to Wales for the return match on 20 May, and although they lost 39-33, Eric was in sparkling form, netting 11 points. Unfortunately, his performances from both meetings were subsequently scrubbed from the records upon the Welsh side's resignation from the league in June. The Aussie was to hit a rich vein of form around his home patch, when he garnered 11 points against Nottingham in a league match on 29 May, and followed it up with successive 12-point maximums against Plymouth and Southampton, the latter match being a Provincial Trophy clash. Away from home, things went well too, with a full maximum being gleaned in a league match at Liverpool on 15 June, followed by a 10-point tally at Nottingham in the Provincial Trophy. On 3 July, Knowle Stadium hosted what would turn out to be the second of five challenge matches that pitched Bristol against America, and the homesters rode their hearts out to win 62-43, with Eric tallying a brilliant 13 points. July ended with totals of 11+1 (paid maximum) and 8+1, against West Ham Hawks in the Provincial Trophy and Liverpool in the league respectively, with the tall scoring continuing unabated into the following month.

Bristol first used their famous Bulldogs nickname at Knowle on 7 August, and Eric was on board to mark the momentous occasion in his own special way. The track record had been lowered several times since the opening meeting of the season, but the flying Queenslander fairly blitzed around in the opening heat to set a new best of 69.2 seconds, prior to ending the night with a haul of 10 points in a 43-29 league success over Nottingam.

There were two more 12-point maximums as the season meandered to its close, when he repeated his earlier season's efforts against Southampton and Plymouth, meaning all that both sets of visiting riders saw of Eric during their league visits to Knowle was his rear wheel! In between those two performances, he amazingly notched yet another full-house against Southampton, when the Bristol boys travelled to Banister Court for a Provincial Trophy fixture on 17 September, and came away with a 40-29 win under their belts. Six days before that, he achieved his highest score of the year, in another one of Bristol's challenges with America, when he totalled 16 points in a 63-43 victory. Over the course of the season, Eric was absent from a handful of matches when his parent club, Wimbledon, required him in the higher sphere of racing, but he only missed one league match for the Bulldogs, although crucially, it was the Championship decider at Southampton on 24 September, when the Hampshire men clinched the title, albeit on race points difference, with a 41½-29½ success.

So Bristol had to settle for second position at the end of an excellent first campaign, and it was no surprise to see Eric's name at the head of their scoring list, as he had bagged 126 points from 15 league matches; his nearest challenger, Harry Shepherd, was a couple of dozen points behind.

After his outstanding year sporting the black and orange race-jacket, the fans and management looked forward to him again leading the Bulldogs attack in 1937. But Eric was a victim of his own success, as Wimbledon wanted him on a full-time basis. No one could really blame them though, since he had given his all for Bristol; and he was to fully justify the Londoners decision too, registering 155 points for an average of 6.88, having remained ever-present throughout their 24-match league programme.

Sadly, he suffered from inconsistency in 1938, and although he again completed a full quota of 24 league matches for the Dons, his points total fell to 110, yielding an average of just 5.74. Thankfully, the last season of pre-war activity saw him regain his touch for the Plough Lane club, and with 134 points from 17 fixtures, he boasted an impressive top-flight average of 8.53, when the sport was brought to a premature stop. The year had also seen Eric accumulate 30 points in the championship round, thereby gaining a spot in the World Final, with 4 bonus points carried forward.

Having missed out on the Star Championship final in 1932, due to injury, he had been looking forward to the big night at Wembley. However, the outbreak of war meant this was never to be. The hostilities brought an end to his career, so he never got another chance to grace the individual stage; however, he did at least represent his country internationally in four Test match series versus England (1936-39), as well as racing for the Aussies against the Provincial League in 1937. On top of that, Eric also rode against England for both the Overseas in 1937, and the Dominions in 1938 and 1939. Despite his time with Bristol spanning just the one season, he always squared up to the opposition and was most definitely the top Bulldog during their historic first year of league activity.

Competition	Matches	Points
League	30	125
National Trophy	5	5
Provincial League KOC	4	41
Southern Shield	6	11
Western Cup	4	31
Challenge	13	40
4 Team Tournament	1	8
Mini-Matches	5	15
Bulldogs Total	**68**	**276**

Clifford Cox was born on 8 March 1933, at Stanton Drew, and followed in a long line of local boys who rode for Bristol – a fine tradition indeed. His racing career began in 1952, and he was to endure a long, hard and often disappointing time, before finally becoming a heat-leader.

When he signed his contract for the club, Bristol promoter George Allen was under the impression that the young man seated before him was called Fred Cox, and it was only when he put pen to paper that his new boss realized the mistake! Despite his in-experience, Cliff was to ride in two league matches for the Bulldogs in 1952, the first of which occurred on 12 September when he appeared against Odsal (Bradford), at Knowle Stadium.

This came about due to a late call-up for Dick Bradley to ride for England in a Test match against Australia at Harringay, and Cliff did at least manage to mark the occasion of his club debut with a solitary point. In 1953 he rode mostly in second-half events and mini-matches, although he did get to appear in the first team for three away league fixtures at Birmingham, Harringay and Odsal. It certainly wasn't easy for a young novice

amidst the cut and thrust of Division One racing, but Cliff put in plenty of effort even though he failed to register any points. One performance of note that year, however, was against Swindon in a mini-match at Knowle on 29 May, when he took victory in both his outings for a 6-point tally, as the Bulldogs claimed a 10-2 success.

The following year, when Bristol competed in Division Two racing, it seemed there would be more opportunities for Cliff, particularly since one or two members of the side appeared to be just 'going through the motions', but surprisingly it wasn't to be. He didn't get to ride in a single league fixture, his outings being limited to 3 National Trophy matches, and 6 in the Southern Shield.

Things did improve in 1955, when he got 7 first-team matches under his belt in the league, only for Bristol to close down in June, having failed to attract sufficient numbers through the turnstiles. Little was heard of

Cliff following the Bulldogs demise, until he re-appeared with Oxford in 1959, and represented the Cheetahs second side in several Reserve League matches.

Unfortunately, the league ended in disarray, with the fixtures incomplete, but at least it had given Cliff the chance of kick-starting his 'shale-shifting' career. Aside from his stint at Oxford, he also rode for Bristol in two challenge matches at Knowle, the sport having returned to the venue with a short run of open-licence meetings.

During the winter, important things happened, which proved to be the saviour of speedway, and allowed riders like Cliff Cox the opportunity to make good. The ten-team Provincial League was formed, with one of the competing sides being Bristol, who were happy to return to regular racing following the success of their open-licence events the previous year. Headed by skipper Johnny Hole, a useful team was assembled, with Cliff happy to be amongst the starting line-up. He had worked hard to establish himself in the sport, with little joy, but this was an ideal situation, and he was to grab it with both hands. In the event, the Bulldogs were unlucky not to finish the season as League Champions, having instead to settle for third place in the final table, due to losing home matches against Rayleigh and Poole - the two sides that finished above them! Although Cliff rode well at home, the highlights being 11 points against Sheffield, and 10 versus Poole, he was even better on his travels, gleaning 12-point maximums at both Odsal and Liverpool, plus scores of paid 11 (8+3) at Sheffield, and paid 10 (8+2) at Rayleigh. He remained ever-present throughout the 18-match campaign, with his season's tally being an impressive 119 points; and emphasizing just how good he was away from Knowle, 67 of that total were garnered on the road.

Any disappointment at not winning the league title was quickly forgotten, when the men in orange and black went on to win the Knock-Out Cup. Having journeyed to West Yorkshire, and comfortably dismissed Odsal 61-35, the Bulldogs then travelled to Edinburgh, and romped to a 58-38 semi-final success, with Cliff racing to a brilliant paid maximum (14+1) in typically spectacular fashion. That brought them face to face with League Champions Rayleigh in a two-legged final, with the Essex side staging the first match on 9 September. A tense affair ensued, but it was the homesters who managed to eke out a 52-41 win, with Cliff's contribution for the Bulldogs being a valuable 6 points. The return match, and incidentally what turned out to be the last-ever meeting at Knowle Stadium, duly took place on 23 September, when Cliff registered 14 points as the Bristol boys produced an inspired performance to win 59-37 on the night, and more importantly, 100-89 on aggregate.

Having performed very well in the qualifying rounds, Cliff rode in the Provincial League Riders' Championship final at Cradley Heath the evening immediately following the cup glory, but he endured a nightmare, failing to trouble the scorers. With Bristol shut, he then linked with Plymouth for two brilliant seasons, scoring 158 league points in 1961, followed by another 206 in 1962. Sadly, Plymouth then closed down, with Cliff subsequently joining Exeter in 1963, when his sparkling form continued as he accumulated 181 league points. Disaster was to strike in 1964, however, when having netted 40 points for the Falcons, he suffered a badly broken leg in a track crash. The injury took time to heal, and he was to only appear in three league matches for Exeter in the debut season of the British League in 1965. He then seemed lost to the sport, but surprisingly made a brief comeback with the re-opened Plymouth in 1969, riding in only a handful of matches.

The programme from Cliff Cox's Bristol debut against Odsal (Bradford) on 12 September 1952.

Competition	Matches	Points
League	37	85
National Trophy	5	20
Provincial Trophy	1	6
English Speedway Trophy	4	4
Union Cup	2	2
British Speedway Cup	11	45
Challenge	9	40
Bulldogs Total	**69**	**202**

George Godfrey Craig was born in Deptford, South-East London on 6 June 1915, and it was as a supporter of New Cross that he first became interested in speedway racing.

He eventually joined the Old Kent Road outfit in 1939, having impressed their management the year before when he took his first 'skids' at Dagenham. George didn't make any appearances for New Cross, their bosses preferring for him to gain experience by loaning him out to Bristol, who were then a Division Two outfit. He duly made his debut for the club in an English Speedway Trophy encounter with Hackney Wick at Knowle on 2 May, ending the match with a single point to his name. It took George time to settle, and points were hard to come by, but he was to finally hit peak form when he knocked up 8+1 points in a home Division Two match against Sheffield on 25 August.

That proved to be the last meeting at Knowle before the outbreak of war, and took his league total to 33 points from 12 matches. Although he subsequently appeared in a Provincial Trophy match at Belle Vue five days later, sadly, there was to an elongated gap in his career, just when he appeared to be on the threshold of great things. However, at least he was able to keep his hand in with motorcycles during the hostilities, since he became a dispatch rider in the Royal Corps of Signals.

Following his war service, George returned in 1946, to ride for Bristol once again. At the time, the club were running a series of open-licence meetings, with a view to staging league racing in 1947. Having returned to the team in late September, he was to only race in four meetings, but he did well to net a total of 30 points, including a tally of 10+3 against a composite side of Northern League Stars on 4 October. The Bulldogs did indeed return to regular league racing in 1947, resuming in Division Two with a side that contained many local boys, and as such, added to the interest of the thousands of supporters who flocked through the Knowle turnstiles on a weekly basis. George became a regular in the line-up, but by and large the good form he had shown the previous year seemed to desert him. He looked good in a home match against Glasgow on 16 May, when he recorded 8+2 points in a 57½-26½ victory, but the end of season statistics told their own story, with a total of only 52 league points from 25 matches.

In 1948, George was transferred to Hull, a side new to Division Three racing, with the princely sum of £90 changing hands for his services. The somewhat unexpected move was to do him the world of good, for he settled well on his new D-shaped home circuit and having registered 280 league points, he become the Angels second highest scorer behind Mick Mitchell.

So to 1949 and George continued with the East Yorkshire outfit until they were forced to close down prematurely, due to insufficient attendance levels. At the time, he had accumulated another 170 league points. However, his season didn't end there as he subsequently accompanied team-mates Mick Mitchell, Derek Glover and Alf Webster to Swindon. The Wiltshire track had only opened a few weeks earlier in July, and with George's former Bristol boss Reg Witcomb at the helm, the Robins were only too happy to take over the defunct side's outstanding fixtures. George duly made his debut for the Robins in what was their historic first league match at Poole on 5 September, when he notched 5 points in a 53-31 defeat. Swindon only completed 13 league fixtures at the tail-end of that year, but George appeared in them all, scoring a very useful 85 points for an average of 6.69.

Remaining with the Robins in 1950, he was to ride in 35 Division Three matches, collecting 201 points for a marginally lower average of 6.26. Despite this slight reduction in his end-of-term figure, it came as a real shock to Swindon supporters when Reg Witcomb released the popular teamster during the winter.

Surprisingly, it took a little while for George to get fixed up with a new club, and for a short spell in 1951, he ended up helping the Robins when they suffered injury problems, appearing in a single National Trophy tie, plus four matches in the Festival of Britain Trophy. It was in the latter competition that George really thrilled the Blunsdon faithful with a paid maximum (12+3 points) against Long Eaton on 28 April, his team riding with old partner Bob Jones being a joy to behold on the night.

He eventually secured a team spot with Plymouth for the rest of the season, scoring a total of 93 league points, before disappearing from the sport. Indeed, nothing was heard from George for a number of years until he wrote a letter to the late Ron Hoare, then secretary of the Veteran Riders' Association. In it, he proudly stated how he had emigrated to Perth, Australia and was enjoying a new sport, namely skydiving, at seventy-plus years of age! Some years later, George came over to 'Blighty' to catch up with members of his family, and while here, it was only natural that he should contact former team-mate Bob Jones and make a pilgrimage to see a meeting at the Abbey Stadium, where the crowd gave him a most warm welcome back.

A great character was George Craig, and with a fine sense of fun, he enjoyed a marvellous relationship with the fans who flocked to speedway. There was never a dull moment when he was around, and wherever he raced, he left a host of happy memories. Today, well into his eighties, George is still throwing himself out of aeroplanes from a height of around 3,000 metres, and has notched up over 800 jumps.

Competition	Matches	Points
League	21	86
Inter-League KOC	1	2
Challenge	4	11
Bulldogs Total	**26**	**99**

Bruce Brian Hoani Cribb was born in Palmerston North, New Zealand on 27 June 1946, and whilst at school he was something of an all-round sportsman, playing cricket and rugby, as well as also enjoying both swimming and athletics.

His shale career began at his local track in 1963, and two seasons later, he followed the path of legendary Kiwi aces Ronnie Moore, Barry Briggs and Ivan Mauger when he came to the United Kingdom to race. His arrival in this country coincided with the first year of the newly-formed British League, and with the season already under way, it was fellow New Zealander Bill Andrew who suggested to his bosses at Poole that they took an in-depth look at the young 'Cribby'. In the beginning, he had to adjust to the riding conditions here, since they were so very different to those he had been used to. However, he was young, keen as mustard, and willing to both listen and learn. After making a scoreless debut in a

home match against Edinburgh on 4 August, he went on to make 10 league appearances for the Pirates, scoring 15 points, and whilst these figures weren't particularly outstanding, they did suggest the promise of better things to come.

That proved to be exactly what happened, and Bruce was to remain with Poole until the end of 1969, a season which saw him appear in each and every one of the 36 league meetings, and play a major role as the Pirates won the British League Championship. Indeed, he showed all the signs of becoming a heat-leader as he tallied 227 points for an average of 7.29, lending great support to Pete Smith, Geoff Mudge, Odd Fossengen and Gordon Guasco.

Despite that success, he was on the move to Exeter in 1970, and the wanderlust was to become a feature of his riding career. Bruce showed great form around the huge County Ground bowl, and was to finish his first year as a Falcon boasting a league average of 9.31.

Although he didn't scale the dizzy heights of a 9+ average again with Exeter, a further two seasons were spent with the Devon outfit, before he was on the move again, linking with Cradley Heath. His best campaign with the Heathens occurred in 1976, when he remained ever-present to achieve a league average of 7.77, having accumulated 288 points. During his time with the West Midlanders, 'Cribby' first donned a Bristol race-jacket when failing to score as a guest in an away league match at Hull on 13 July 1977.

The following year he was still a regular in the Cradley Heath line-up, when a surprise mid-season change saw him join Bristol for a reported £4,000 transfer fee. His first meeting as a full-time Bulldog was at Eastville on 30 June, when he recorded 8 points, and helped his new team to a narrow 40-38 win over King's Lynn in a Gulf British League encounter. Whereas many riders would often complain about the Bristol circuit, the Kiwi just went out and raced, whatever the conditions. In spite of this, some of his scoring was a bit indifferent for the Bulldogs, but there were also several inspirational Eastville performances, including 8+1 points in a 45-33 victory against Hackney Wick on 29 August, and a brilliant paid maximum (10+2) as his side ran riot to swamp Reading 55-23 on 6 October. When the 1978 season came to a close, Bruce had 86 points, and an average of 5.32 to his name from 20 league matches in the Bristol colours, and the supporters looked forward to again seeing him in action at 'tapes-up' the following year.

However, the club was beset with problems, and on 18 December the news came that the best supported track in Britain was no more. That meant another move for the New Zealander, and having joined Wolverhampton for 1979, he raced in 32 league matches for 167 points and a 5.94 average. A real highlight that year saw the legendary Ivan Mauger lead New Zealand to glory in the World Team Cup Final at London's White City Stadium on 16 September. Bruce certainly played his part in their success, notching a 5-point tally.

Again the Kiwi raced for Wolverhampton in 1980, and also made some late-season appearances for Oxford in the National League. With the Wolves subsequently dropping into the National League themselves in 1981, an upsurge in form saw 'Cribby' net 345½ points for a high 9.96 average, while also 'doubling-up' on several occasions with Birmingham. He then linked with Berwick at their new Berrington Lough home in 1982, and was to remain with the Borders outfit for four years until the end of 1985, during which time he continued to take fleeting British League outings with Birmingham (1982-83) and Reading (1984). Bruce certainly enjoyed his spell with the Bandits, riding in a total of 135 league matches, and scoring 1,294 points in the process, with his best season being 1984, when he posted a 9.13 average.

Aside from the odd match in the British League, he was to see out his racing days with a three year stint back at Exeter (1986-88), during which he raced in 45 league matches for 370 points, with the last couple of seasons being particularly hampered by injury. During his elongated service to the sport, Bruce not only performed at international level for his native New Zealand, but also Great Britain, the Rest of the World, and Australasia, as well as Scotland at National League level! He was also an accomplished ice racer, and there was no more a thrilling sight than the Kiwi mounted on his spike-tyred machine, when shattering track records in demonstration rides at conventional shale circuits.

He was certainly a tough character, and this was fully emphasized once in a match at Exeter, when he was involved in a first bend pile-up. He got to his feet, but the St John Ambulance staff quickly established that he'd dislocated a shoulder. That didn't worry Bruce however, as he promptly walked back to the pits, caught hold of the beam in the covered area, and gently turned around until his shoulder went back into place with a loud crack. That done, he had a quick word with his team manager, and was out for the re-run, which he duly won!

Competition	Matches	Points
League	59	658
Knock-Out Cup	6	74
Inter-League KOC	5	49
Spring Gold Cup	12	125
Challenge	10	112
4 Team Tournament	11	92
Bulldogs Total	**103**	**1,110**

Philip John Crump was born on 9 February 1952, at Red Cliffs, Mildura, Australia, and was most certainly one of the greatest Australian speedway riders of all-time. His career began in after meeting practice at Mildura in November 1970, and he made such rapid progress that in 1971, he was recommended to try his luck in this country.

He was fortunate enough to meet up with Neil Street, one of Australia's great gifts to England, who helped Phil, advised him, and became his mentor. The youngster listened and learned, before accepting an offer from Maury Littlechild, the promoter of Crewe, whose side had joined Division Two of the British League in 1969. It was felt that the huge Crewe circuit, constructed around the old LMR Cricket Ground, with fast, sweeping bends, would suit the Mildura man, as another Australian import, Geoff Curtis, had previously mastered the Earle Street bowl during the 1969 season. Phil was quick to settle in at his new home, and his progress was

such that by the end of his first British campaign, he had posted a league average of 8.93, having accumulated 283 points. Many Division One clubs had noted his high scoring, and as such, Phil also enjoyed a number of guest bookings in the top-flight.

To be fair though, he didn't score too many points at that level, but the experience did him the world of good. He remained with Crewe in 1972, and it was a year when he became almost unbeatable, not just around his home track, but also on pretty much every away raceway as well. Along with John Jackson and Garry Flood, he formed a potent spearhead as Crewe completed a marvellous double success, winning the League Championship and Knock-Out Cup. With 375 points to his name, Phil's end of season average shot up to a massive 11.10 figure, as he appeared in each and every one of the Kings 32-match league programme, and headed the entire figures in his sphere of racing. Capping a wonderful year, he was crowned Division Two Riders' Champion at Wimbledon on 14 October, having defeated Arthur Price in a run-off after both had notched dozen point tallies.

Again, he took several bookings in Division One throughout the season, and it was obvious that Phil would move up on a full-time basis in 1973. One of the side's he had ridden for was King's Lynn, scoring 113 points from 17 league matches, and as they were also promoted by

Maury Littlechild, it was only natural that he should link with the Norfolk outfit. However, it unfortunately became a season that Phil wasn't able to look back on with any fond memories. Everything went wrong on 7 April, when he suffered a puncture whilst travelling home after scoring 7 points in a Border Trophy match against visiting Leicester. He stopped to change the tyre, only for the car jack to slip, leaving him with a crushed hand and his season at a premature end. At the time, he had participated in just one league match at Oxford two nights previously, netting 3+1 points.

Thankfully, the tough Aussie made a full recovery, and in 1974, began a love affair with Newport, teaming up alongside Neil Street, who by then had become his father-in-law. The Welsh track had its critics amongst the riders, but it made no difference to Phil, who simply went out and rode it (and every other circuit) quite brilliantly. In what was effectively his first full season in the top division, he thundered to 364 points for an average of 10.77, with only the big three of Ole Olsen, Ivan Mauger and Peter Collins finishing on higher league figures.

Amazingly, he increased both his scoring to 386 points, and average to 11.17 the following year, as Newport climbed up to third spot in the re-titled British League table, behind Ipswich and Belle Vue. The year also saw 'Crumpie' make it to his first World Final at Wembley Stadium on 6 September, when he won his first two heats, and went on to score 10 points in a highly impressive showing. In 1976, he did even better, notching a dozen points to occupy third position on the World Final rostrum at Katowice, Poland on 5 September. Meanwhile, on the domestic front, it was his last season with Newport, and his haul of league points totalled 434 for another substantial average of 10.69.

Despite their well-balanced team, the crowds were disappointing at the Welsh venue, and it really came as no surprise when promoters John Richards and Wally Mawdsley transferred their operation to a new 390 metre circuit at Bristol, situated around Bristol Rovers' football pitch at Eastville Stadium, actually on the existing greyhound racing strip! As such, the track did cause

problems to a number of riders, and many complained about it, but not Phil Crump, who had been elected skipper of the new Bulldogs. He just took things in his stride and got on with the job of scoring points for his new club, having made his debut with a 12 point tally from 5 starts in a league match at Wolverhampton on 1 April. That set the tone for the year, and it was a case of regular double-figure scores at home, and much the same on his travels. 'Crumpie' led by example before the huge crowds that flocked to Eastville Stadium, netting league maximums against Coventry (12), Leicester (11+1), Reading (12) and Hull (12), as well as a further six unbeaten scores in other team matches. On the road, he also netted full-house totals at Exeter (15) in the Spring Gold Cup, at Wimbledon (14+1) in the league, and at Hull (15) in the Knock-Out Cup, and was clearly enjoying a productive year – when disaster struck at a rain-soaked Sheffield in the semi-final of the Gauloises British League Pairs Championship on 15 September.

Unfortunately, the Australian was involved in a track accident with Swindon ace Martin Ashby, which left him with a broken right leg. With his season brought to a premature close, Phil's league statistics revealed a total of 260 points from 24 matches for an average of 9.49.

Happily, he recovered to line-up for the Bulldogs in 1978, when the points again flowed in abundance. So much so, in fact, that his haul of 398 points from 35 matches was the highest attained by any rider in the Gulf British League. That gave him a final average of 9.99, helped in no small way by home maximums against Wimbledon (15), Wolverhampton (11+1), Hull (11+1), Ipswich (15) and Belle Vue (12), plus an away one at Swindon (15) on 29 July.

Sadly, storm clouds were gathering over Bristol, and a legal battle developed to keep the sport at Eastville, which was ultimately lost in December, some six week's after the season's end. As a result, Phil and fellow Bulldog Steve Gresham moved with promoter Wally Mawdsley to Swindon, where the Aussie became the linchpin of the Robins side, accumulating no less than 1,977 points from 185 league matches from 1979-86 inclusive.

During that time, he made his third and last World Final appearance, scoring 4 points at the Memorial Coliseum in Los Angeles on 28 August. He also celebrated a much-deserved Testimonial for ten years service under the Wally Mawdsley promoting banner (Newport 1974-76, Bristol 1977-78 and Swindon 1979-83), with his special meeting staged at Blunsdon on 2 October 1983.

Sadly, 'Crumpie' retired from the British scene at the end of the 1986 season owing to a long-standing wrist injury. He did make a comeback in 1990, however, and the crowds at Blunsdon immediately increased, but unfortunately at the age of nearly 39, much of the old magic had waned and he could only glean 63 league points from 16 matches. Nevertheless, Phil Crump was a great speedway rider, being a real racer and a team manager's dream. He was always prepared to take an extra outing, and two or even three rides on the trot when required to do so. Whatever the opposition, he just went out and raced, always doing his very best.

Competition	Matches	Points
League	61	328½
National Trophy	10	71
Provincial Trophy	14	107
ACU Cup	6	16
Coronation Cup	4	34
English Speedway Trophy	6	39
Union Cup	2	6
Challenge	25	132
Mini-Matches	1	4
Bulldogs Total	**129**	**737½**

Roy Dook was born in London on 23 August 1907, and was a rider of considerable experience when he linked with Bristol upon the return of the sport to the City in 1936. He arrived on loan from New Cross, together with Harry Shepherd, and Bristol boss Ronnie Greene was quick to acknowledge the help he had received from his counterpart at the London club, Fred Mockford, in putting his side together.

Roy was one of the dirt-track pioneers in 1928, and he was to become one of the sport's frequent travellers. After beginning his league career at Lea Bridge in 1929, he spent 1930 at West Ham, prior to resuming at Lea Bridge the following season. He then joined Coventry for two years, and in his first term with the Warwickshire outfit, he made it through to the prestigious Star Championship final, although a second place in the opening heat meant a quick elimination from the event.

Roy was to make New Cross his home in 1934, and he was still on board with the Londoners in 1936, when the opportunity presented itself to also race for Bristol in their initial season of league activity. The first match for the newly-formed team was a Provincial League encounter at Nottingham on 28 April, and things just couldn't have turned out better if they had been scripted. Bristol claimed a marvellous 34-33 victory, and the star of the show was undoubtedly the man who had been elected captain, one Roy Dook. He scorched to a track record of 75.36 seconds for the 380-yard circuit in heat one, before going on to complete a stunning 12-point maximum. Having made such a fine start, Bristol opened their season at Knowle Stadium on 8 May, when Southampton provided the opposition in another league fixture. Like the meeting at Nottingham, it proved to be a closely fought contest, but the West-Countrymen again emerged victorious by 38 points to 32. It was a solid team performance, and with a tally of 8+2 points, Roy was second top scorer behind maximum man Eric Collins. That was to be his best league score around Bristol's tight 290-yard racing strip and he was generally good for more points in away matches. He was, however, a very good skipper, and played his part in ensuring that the side had a fine team spirit running throughout. As and when other commitments would allow, he appeared in a total of 12 league fixtures for the Bulldogs, scoring 68 points in the process, and aside from his full-house at Nottingham the other real high spot was a paid maximum (11+1) at Plymouth on 7 July. Roy did produce several notable showings in other matches over the course of the season, the best of which was 14 points against America in a challenge match at Knowle on 3 July.

With speedway well and truly established in Bristol, Roy became a full-time Bulldog in 1937, and this seemed to inspire him to greater things for he registered a season's total of 153½ points from 19 league matches. Along with Bill Rogers and Harry Shepherd, he formed a potent spearhead as the Bulldogs swept to the Provincial League Championship; and making it that little bit sweeter was the fact that the team who had pipped them for the 1936 title, Southampton, finished 4 points behind them in second spot.

He measurably improved his home form, registering paid maximums against Liverpool (10+2) on 7 May, and Nottingham (11+1) on 28 May. It was fair to say he still generally performed better on the team's travels, however, with four-ride maximums carded at Liverpool (first match) and Nottingham, plus a paid full-house at Norwich (11+1) on 12 June. On top of that, he was paid for maximums (11+1) both at home and away to Leicester. But with the Midlanders resigning from the league after completing just six matches, Roy's total for the year was considerably less than it otherwise would have been.

Over the course of the season, he also went through the card in a Coronation Cup match at Norwich on 15 May, winning all four of his rides and twice breaking the Firs Stadium track-record along the way, while a paid maximum (11+1) was also netted against Nottingham in the same competition at Knowle on 23 July.

The Londoner was happy to stay on board with the Bulldogs upon their elevation into the National League Division One in 1938,

while he also had outings with New Cross Reserves in the English Speedway Trophy. Sadly, it was to be a season of struggle both for him personally, and Bristol. With just six wins, plus one draw from their 24 fixtures, the West Country boys occupied the unwanted basement position in the table, with Roy mustering only 33 points from 16 matches. His difficulty in scoring was emphasized by the fact that at Knowle his best performances of the year were tallies of 3+2 against West Ham and 3+1 versus Harringay. As usual, he fared better away from home, but only marginally, with his best returns being 4 points at Wimbledon, while he was credited with scores of 3+1 at both Harringay and Belle Vue. He did have slightly better luck in other competitions, however, registering totals at Knowle of 7+2 against Belle Vue (ACU Cup) and 6 against West Ham (National Trophy), with his highest score for the term being 8 points in a challenge fixture at Edinburgh on 6 August.

Roy naturally sported the orange and black colours of the Bulldogs upon their subsequent quick return to Division Two the following year, and happily with it, his form came back too. Amazingly, for the only time in his Bristol career, he actually recorded more points around his own patch than he did away! When the season was suddenly brought to a close by the outbreak of war, he had accumulated a total 74 league points from 14 matches, with his best tallies being 11 at Norwich on 10 June, and 10+1 against the same opposition when they visited the Bulldogs' home thirteen days later. As a team, however, Bristol weren't doing much better than the season before at the time of the cessation of activities, for they were lying fifth out of six teams, following the earlier withdrawals of both Middlesbrough and Crystal Palace. Prior to their closure, Roy had enjoyed several good meetings against Crystal Palace, netting 9 points in a league match at the London venue, as well as home and away scores of 10+2, and 12+1 respectively in the National Trophy, plus home and away totals of 10+1, and 8+1 in the English Speedway Trophy.

Following the war he joined Birmingham in 1946, racing for them in the Northern League and heading their scoring with 145 points. Roy remained with the Brummies for a further two

years and then went into management, being identified with Rayleigh in 1949. He later moved on to act as technical adviser at Newcastle in 1951, and when things were tough for his team, he again donned his leathers to help out. Roy accumulated 24 points from the league matches he appeared in, but his efforts couldn't help the club from avoiding the wooden spoon in the Division Two table, or indeed from closing down after the season had ended. At international level, Roy made appearances for the Provincial League against Australia in 1937, and for England versus the Dominions two years later in 1939.

Competition	Matches	Points
League	24	152½
National Trophy	2	16
ACU Cup	6	35
Challenge	6	31½
Bulldogs Total	**38**	**235**

Victor John Duggan was born on 5 September 1910, in West Maitland, New South Wales, Australia. The story goes that Vic began his working life as a Telegraph messenger boy (this no doubt being his first association with motorcycles), and later became a motor mechanic, repairing and maintaining machines.

Vic, it seems, was one of that rare breed of riders who could be described as a 'natural', since after just a few months practice in 1937, he was competing at the Speedway Royale Stadium in Sydney, prior to arriving on these shores to ride for Hackney Wick. He quickly settled to racing in the UK, ending his first season with 17 league appearances and 50 points under his belt for the Wolves, as the London outfit were known in those days. Having suffered from disappointing attendance figures, Hackney's management eventually decided that a drop down to Division Two would be beneficial in 1938,

with Bristol moving in the opposite direction to replace them in the top-flight. As a consequence, Vic, together with team-mates Cordy Milne, Morian Hansen and Bill Clibbett linked with the Bulldogs, who obviously needed strengthening for the higher grade of racing.

The man from West Maitland duly made his debut for Bristol against New Cross in a challenge match at Knowle on 15 April, scoring 4 points in a hefty 62-43 defeat. That result served notice that the West Country side still lacked the necessary strength in depth, and as things panned out, gathering points for his new team initially proved tough for Vic. However, he showed a marvellous fighting spirit and it was interesting to note just how he progressed over the year. In the main, when the opposition made their first league visit of the year to Knowle Stadium, his points reflected the difficulty in adjusting to the pace of Division One racing; yet on the second trip west, the Bulldogs opponents often encountered a different Vic Duggan. He'd grasped the fastest route around the 290-yard circuit and made sure everyone remembered his name. Perfect examples of his home scoring saw him net 5+2 points against Harringay first time around, but this had jumped to 11 for the second match. Against Wembley, he followed up 4 points with a tally of 10. Against Belle Vue he initially recorded 6+1 points, then 9+1 etc., etc. It was much the same on Bristol's travels as he became more accustomed to the differing circuits, his best performances being 9 point totals at both

Harringay and Wembley on his second visit to each. In fact, only against West Ham at home, and New Cross away did the Aussie actually attain less points in the second match.

At the end of the campaign, Vic had totalled 152½ points from the full quota of 24 league matches, with only Cordy Milne finishing on a higher figure in the Bulldogs scorechart. Although he failed to garner a maximum, he was close on several occasions, not least when he scored 11 points against Harringay as previously mentioned, with the same total also being reached against New Cross. Unfortunately Bristol completed the season occupying the bottom position in Division One, having attained just 13 points; however, the development of Vic Duggan at least gave the Knowle faithful something to cheer about.

After a year which could only be described as disastrous as far as the Bulldogs were concerned, it was confirmed in March 1939 that they would be dropping down to compete in Division Two. That meant a parting of the ways for Bristol and Vic, with Wimbledon delightedly stepping in to acquire the services of the super Aussie.

As a member of the Dons, he really blossomed into one of the sport's leading riders, and had amassed 192 points from 18 league matches for an average of 10.67, when proceedings were brought to an abrupt halt by the advent of war. With the World Final also scrapped as a result of the hostilities, Vic was robbed of making his debut in the big event, having been one of the leading qualifiers with 45 points from the championship round.

He subsequently went home to his native land and didn't return to Britain until 1947, when, together with Frank Dolan and brother Ray, he lined-up for Harringay, who were re-opening to Division One speedway. Quite simply, Vic put together a season never to be

forgotten, plundering 275 points (plus 2 bonus) from 24 league matches for an astounding 11.54 average, and hitting no less than 16 full maximums along the way! Meanwhile, in the British Riders' Championship, he didn't drop a point in the preliminary round, and though a hot favourite for the title, he only mustered 8 points in the big event. He made up for his disappointment the following year, however, when taking victory with 14 points, being beaten only by Alec Statham of Wimbledon.

Still based at Harringay in 1948, he notched up another 229 points in the league, and this high-scoring form continued for the Racers in 1949 (326 points) and 1950 (269 points). Surprisingly, his only appearance in the World Final occurred in 1950, when he recorded just a 4 point tally. It was fortunate for speedway in this country that Vic appeared at all that year, since in a tragic accident at the Sydney Showground on 20 January, his brother Ray (who also rode for Bristol in 3 challenge matches in 1938) and Exeter's Norman Clay were both killed in the sport's only double fatality. One can understand how this must have affected Vic, and it must have taken a tremendous amount of courage to give speedway another year, before returning home and retiring.

One very interesting point regarding the speedster is that even his machine was as well known as he was. It was named the 'Black Duck', and when parked in the pits, other riders, mechanics and promoters used to gaze fondly upon it, wondering just what secrets it held. However, it was Swindon's Bob Jones, who had previously been a post-war novice at Bristol, who best summed up the situation. 'It was a darn good bike, looked after and well maintained' said 'Joner'. 'But when they looked at it, they were inclined to forget that the bloke on board was a bit special too', he concluded.

Competition	Matches	Points
League	8	30
Provincial Trophy	5	19
Challenge	5	8
Bulldogs Total	**18**	**57**

Michael Erskine was born in Westbury, Wiltshire, on 22 August 1913, and was once, quite correctly, described as a serious student of the speedway game. This would aptly befit a man who was educated at Eton, one of the most famous of this country's public schools. In addition, Mike received an excellent education in engineering, training as a tool maker, and his skills were to be respected within the world of speedway for many, many years.

His introduction to the sport was at Coventry in 1933, and one of his fellow novices was Alec Statham, who would later be one of his team-mates at Wimbledon between 1948-50. Mike didn't manage to break into the Coventry side, and in 1934, he moved to New Cross, where he gained experience in the Reserve League. Some open-licence outings followed at Luton in 1935, as he continued on his learning curve,

and he also made his full league debut with New Cross later that season.

He remained with the Old Kent Road team in 1936, while gaining extra rides by 'doubling-up' with Provincial League Bristol. His first meeting for the West Country side occurred on 8 May when Southampton provided the opposition in a league fixture at Knowle Stadium, and although the homesters claimed a 38-32 victory, Mike unfortunately failed to trouble the scorers. However, when Cardiff travelled to Bristol a week later on 15 May, it was a very different story, because not only did the men in orange and black win 38-33, but Mike had a marvellous evening, topping their scorechart with 11 points. It is sad to relate that this hard-earned tally wasn't included in the end of term statistics, since Cardiff later resigned from the league, with their results struck from the records. Mike and his team-mates were, of course, paid for their efforts on the night, but he never again quite showed the form for Bristol that he did against the Welsh outfit. Nevertheless, he continued to make strides, notching scores of 6+2 and 6+1 in successive weeks against Liverpool and Nottingham in league encounters at Knowle on 22 May and 29 May.

On 5 June, the man from Wiltshire netted 5 points as Bristol took their winning streak to five out of five in league encounters at home, courtesy of a 40-32 success over Plymouth. This run was abruptly halted a week later though, when Southampton visited for a Provincial Trophy tie, and left victorious by 38 points to 32. It was a weakened Bristol side which took to the track for the match, as Mike was absent due to illness, while both

Roy Dook and Harry Shepherd had to ride for their 'first claim' team New Cross in a National Trophy match at Hackney Wick. It is easy to comment after the event, but if they had been at full strength, or if just Mike had been fit to ride, there is little doubt Bristol would have won.

Anyway, he was soon back in action, and a highlight was the 52-19 trouncing of Liverpool in a home league meeting on 31 July, when he raced to a marvellous paid maximum of 8+4 points. Come the end of the campaign, the Bulldogs, as they had become known in August, only just missed out on the league title to Southampton, purely on race points difference, both sides having won 10 of their 16 matches. Mike's contribution was 30 points from 8 matches, although he was also a non-riding reserve for an away match at Southampton on 24 September.

It was a great surprise when Mike took a break from the sport in 1937, but he was tempted back by Southampton in 1938, when he made 6 Division Two appearances for 15 points. Although still attached to the Hampshire club in 1939, he didn't gain any league outings, instead having to wait until the cessation of hostilities to kick-start his career in earnest when allocated to Wimbledon in 1946.

With the Dons, his partnership with the great Norman Parker became renowned throughout the sport, as the pair thrilled the crowds with some wonderful team riding. Mike began in a quiet fashion, recording 82 points from 16 league matches in that first year with the Londoners, raising his tally to 100 points from 21 meetings in 1947, as the side climbed to third place in the table.

In 1948, his form slipped back a little and he totalled 85 points from 20 Division One fixtures, but although the Dons ended up occupying the unwanted basement position a year later, Mike's form was a revelation as he remained ever-present throughout the 42-match league programme to plunder $261\frac{1}{2}$ points. His efforts were recognized internationally when he was one of the reserves for England in the second Test match versus Australia at Birmingham, although in the event he failed to get a ride.

Mike didn't make a World Final proper, although he was reserve in 1950, actually taking one ride in which he failed to score. That same year saw his league form unfortunately fall away for Wimbledon, as he gleaned 118 points from 30 league matches, and ended the campaign in a reserve berth.

His final season of racing was to be in 1951, when he made 12 league appearances for the Dons, netting just 21 points. Thankfully, Mike wasn't lost to the game, and subsequently used his engineering skills to make a name for himself, having perfected a speedway frame known as the 'Erskine Staride'. These were used and approved by many riders, including Freddie Williams, who was mounted on board one when he took World Championship glory in 1950, and again in 1953. Mike also had a spell as a team manager, when Charlie Knott senior reopened Southampton to Southern League racing in 1952, and a new generation of young riders were able to benefit from his experience. Several years later, Mike's son Jon also entered the world of speedway, racing for Neath (1962), Long Eaton (1963), Newport (1964-70) and Wolverhampton (1970-73).

Competition	Matches	Points
League	18	57
National Trophy	1	1
Provincial League KOC	3	2
British Speedway Cup	4	10
Southern Shield	1	0
Western Cup	4	15
Challenge	8	33
4 Team Tournament	1	1
Bulldogs Total	**40**	**119**

Having been born in Bristol on 9 April 1915, Frank Evans' first tentative steps on the speedway ladder took place 31 years later in 1946, at his local track in a training school run by former West Ham rider Harold 'Tiger' Stevenson. Bristol had run a series of open-licence meetings that year, and were subsequently allocated a place in the National League Second Division of 1947.

Understandably, Frank found the pace a bit too hot, although after making his debut for the Bulldogs in the team's first away league match of the campaign at Middlesbrough on 10 April (scoring 6 points), he went on to total a creditable 29 points from 10 Division Two matches.

To help gain valuable experience, Frank also had a spell with Division Three side Cradley Heath during the season, his stint yielding 45 league points. Representing Hanley, he remained solely in the Third Division the following year, netting a total of 70 points. Frank spent another season with the Potters in 1949, thoroughly enjoying himself as he notched 149 points and helped them to secure the League Championship.

However, despite staying on board with the promoted side in 1950, Frank didn't make any league outings and eventually dropped back down a division to link with Swindon. His Robins debut took place in a league encounter at Rayleigh on 3 June, and in what was a great start, he scored 10 points and helped his new side to a narrow 42-41 victory. He was to produce several useful scores thereafter, finally ending the campaign with a tally of 141 points for a satisfactory league average of 6.39.

Having proved to be a good signing for Swindon, the 1951 season started well for Frank, with 11 points in the opening home challenge match versus Oxford.

Unfortunately, he was then laid low for a short time by a poisoned hand and upon returning, it took time for him to show his best form. Thankfully, he managed to get back in the groove as emphasized when he dashed to a four-ride maximum in a home league match against Wolverhampton on 26 May. He followed that up with paid full-houses versus Cardiff and Aldershot at Blunsdon, prior to again netting a full dozen when Wolverhampton visited for the second time on 15 August. Frank's consistent riding had caught the eye of the Test match selectors and he duly appeared for the England C team against New Zealand at Aldershot, scoring 3 points. He was then named as reserve against America at Swindon on 14 September, and the loudest cheer of the evening came when he roared away from the tapes to win the final heat, having taken the place of fellow Robins teamster Buster Brown. All in all, it had been a successful year, with Frank upping his average to 7.13, having totalled 210 league points.

The 1952 season was really memorable for Frank, since he was ever-present throughout the 36-match Southern League campaign, and having garnered 265 points, he also topped the Swindon averages on 8.09.

After such a wonderful year, much was expected of Frank in 1953, but sadly it wasn't to be. His form deserted him and he struggled to hold down a team place, with his league average sliding to just 5.18. It therefore surprised no one when he announced his retirement at the end of the season. However, he again donned his leathers the following year to help out a short-handed Bristol side for one league match at Leicester, plus a Southern Shield encounter at home to Oxford, although he failed to register any points in either meeting.

That seemed to be it as far as his racing career was concerned, but amazingly at the age of 45, Frank again came out of retirement to assist Bristol in 1960, when he appeared in seven Provincial League fixtures, scoring 28 points. One match that was particularly memorable occurred at Yarmouth on 28 June, when having lost Roy Taylor in nasty heat-two track crash, Frank came into his own to score 7 points, which helped the Bulldogs to a narrow 36-35 victory. Sadly, Bristol closed down at the end of the season and the promotion moved to Plymouth for 1961. However, yet again, Frank was on hand to help out the re-titled Plymouth Bulldogs, although he only managed to record a couple of league points. Later that year, he finally retired for good, having provided many thrills during his various spells on the track. In another of many family connections the sport has thrown up over the years, Frank's son Richard also represented Swindon for a time during 1977-78 (riding in a total of 12 league matches), and was later co-promoter at Blunsdon in 1998, on behalf of stadium owners, the BS Group.

Competition	Matches	Points
League	15	60
Provincial League KOC	4	23
Western Cup	4	28
Challenge	6	14
4 Team Tournament	2	13
Bulldogs Total	**31**	**138**

Ronald Ernest Flanagan was born in London on 13 September 1925, but was always known simply as Pat. Prior to his interest in speedway, he took a job as a porter at Covent Garden, and like many youngsters before him, his first experience of the cinder sport was at a Rye House training school, with some second-half trials at Harringay.

The one thing all novices need is track time, however, and when, in 1950, he heard that former rider George Saunders had been appointed as manager of Aldershot, he enquired about trials, and having suitably impressed, he signed on for the Shots. The Hampshire outfit were embarking on their first season of Division Three racing at the time, and Pat initially did well, netting 9 points in the opening meeting at the venue, an individual event for the Easter Trophy. Another early highlight was 9+3 points in a National Trophy tie against visiting Poole on 19 April, but unfortunately, he suffered a loss

of form and eventually ended up riding in second-half events, with his tally for the season being 51 league points. In 1951, he tried his luck with Division Three newcomers Long Eaton, but again his best form eluded him, and he only mustered 8 points for the Archers.

A move to Rayleigh followed in 1952, but despite plenty of effort, he still couldn't find any worthwhile form, and having registered just 7 league points, little was heard of Pat for some considerable time. That was until 1957, when he reappeared with Aldershot, who were then members of the 4-team Southern Area League. His return bolstered the side, and he formed a particularly productive partnership with Ron Walton, the duo netting 141 points between them, with Pat's contribution being 68. Although formidable around their own pear-shaped circuit, the Poppies, as they were known that year, lost all six matches on their travels, occupying third place in the final analysis.

Following another year away from the scene, Pat joined Ipswich in 1959, again in the Southern Area League, but in something of a disappointing season, he could only attain 16 points. It was indeed disappointing to a see a rider always as keen as a knife-edge, working so hard to do well in speedway, yet failing to make the progress his efforts deserved.

The Provincial League was formed in 1960, and it would prove to be the biggest boost the sport had enjoyed in years. Some critics unfairly dubbed it a 'comeback' league, but there can be no doubt it became speedway's saviour. True, there were a number of riders who took the opportunity to return to the saddle, but it also provided a launch pad for many youngsters to make good. Bristol were founder members of the new set-up, and they certainly packed their side with experience, with one of the riders taken on being Pat, while another was a former team-mate at Aldershot in 1950, namely Trevor Redmond.

Having had the proposed opener at Knowle Stadium rained-off, the Bulldogs first activity saw them travel to Cradley Heath for a challenge match on 23 April, when both teams fought out a thrilling 36-36 draw, with Pat gleaning 5 points for his new club. Bristol were to have a fabulous year, and although they only just missed out on the League Championship, they went all the way in the Knock-Out Cup to close the season in style. Pat's contribution in the league was 60 points from 15 meetings, with his best performances being wonderful paid maximums on successive weeks at Knowle against Edinburgh (9+3) on 27 May and Liverpool (11+1) on 3 June. Meanwhile, in the Knock-Out Cup, he notched 11+3 points from 6 starts in the first round at Bradford, as the Bulldogs cruised to a 61-35 victory. Then in the semi-final, he scored 4+2 points in a 58-38 win at the Old Meadowbank home of Edinburgh, as the men in orange and black eased into the final. That meant a showdown with Rayleigh over two legs, with Pat failing to register a point as the Essex team claimed a 52-41 success in the first leg at their place on 9 September. Not wishing to end the year empty-handed, the Bristol boys raced to a 59-37 victory in the return match at Knowle on 23 September, with Pat netting a vital 8+1 points. That gave Bristol an aggregate win by 100 points to 89, much to the delight of their supporters.

Unfortunately, there was bad news around the corner for the riders and fans alike, as shortly afterwards, the Bulldogs lost their home to the developers. For 1961 Bristol relocated to Plymouth, taking Pat with them, but having garnered 39 points he moved to

Newcastle in an effort to help establish the Diamonds in their first season of Provincial League racing. Despite knocking-up 49 points for the Geordies, he was unable to prevent his team – who didn't actually join the league until June – from collecting the unwanted 'wooden spoon', having only taken victory in just 5 of their 20 matches.

In 1962, Pat had a brief spell with Ipswich in the National League, but he didn't score a point, with the Suffolk venue subsequently forced to close in mid-season due to falling attendances. A few rides for non-league Weymouth the followed, under the promotion of John Pilblad.

Pat then seemed to drift away from the sport again, until out of the blue, he turned up in Devon as a member of the Exeter septet, replacing the injured Eric Howe in the first leg of the Revenge Bowl against Stoke at the County Ground on 8 April 1963. Although he only scored a couple of points in the match, he impressed sufficiently to warrant a regular team spot in the Falcons Provincial League line-up, and went on to end the year with 44 points to his name.

Staying with the Falcons, Pat recorded just 22 points over the next two seasons with Exeter, after which, he was seemingly lost to the sport. That was until 1968, when he returned to represent Canterbury in the newly-formed British League Division Two, riding under the promotion of the sport's founder Johnnie Hoskins. He made 11 league appearances for the Crusaders, scoring 30 points, and was also in the side for the first leg of the Knock-Out Cup final against Reading, but unfortunately missed the return match when his colleagues completed a fine aggregate success. Pat rode in just two more meetings for Canterbury in 1969, and also made one non-scoring appearance with King's Lynn II, before finally hanging up his leathers for good.

His career in speedway might have spanned a long time, but it was at Bristol where Pat was most successful, and he really enjoyed himself as an important 'back-up' man for the 1960 Bulldogs.

Competition	Matches	Points
League	56	454
Knock-Out Cup	6	57
Inter-League KOC	4	30
Spring Gold Cup	11	81
Challenge	10	77
4 Team Tournament	6	47
Bulldogs Total	**93**	**746**

Steven Richard Gresham was born in Santa Monica, California, USA on 18 August 1954, and was always interested in motorcycle racing throughout his childhood. He first tried his hand at speedway racing aged 15, in 1969, and four years later he finished eleventh in the USA National Championships. Then, in 1974, he had a brief spell in this country with Hull, marking his debut with a 2 point return against Halifax in a Northern Trophy match at the Boulevard on 3 April. Scoring was to prove difficult for the young American, and he then had to endure a spell on the sidelines after suffering a knock to his arm, missing several of the Vikings early league fixtures in the process. Steve regained fitness and a team spot in late June, but after netting 18 points from 5 Division One matches, he suddenly upped sticks and returned to his homeland for the remainder of the year.

Returning to these shores in 1975, he linked with Newport and soon began to find the fastest route around the tricky Somerton Park circuit. Notable early home perform-

ances in the British League included 8+3 points against Swindon on 11 April, and a tally of 9+2 versus Cradley United on 25 April. These showings, and many others that followed, quickly endeared 'Gresh' to the Newport supporters, and through sheer hard work he was to accumulate a season's total of 136 points from 31 league matches for a solid 6.04 average.

Naturally, the Welsh club wanted him back in 1976, and with his all-out racing style he developed into one of the best 'back-up' men in the business, posting a 7.46 average from 32 league matches, having raised his scoring to 252 points.

In 1977, the Newport promotion moved their top-flight operation to the well-appointed Eastville Stadium in Bristol, with Steve accompanying team-mates Phil Crump, Phil Herne and Tormod Langli to the new venture. Unfortunately, a pre-season incident back in the States saw his wife, Cathy, injured by an assailant. This clearly wasn't the ideal preparation for a hard term of racing. In view of that, it was hardly surprising when he failed to trouble the scorers on his Bristol debut in a Spring Gold Cup encounter at Exeter on 4 April, but he soon settled down and the points began to flow.

As he had done at Newport, Steve was to become very popular with the new breed of

Bulldogs fans. He was completely fearless, reputations meant nothing to him, and his no-nonsense riding had everyone up on their toes, or on the edge of their seats. With its sandy surface, the Bulldogs 390-metre home strip was unusual to say the least, and as Steve adapted to the surroundings, a particularly impressive showing occurred in a Knock-Out Cup tie against Wimbledon on 17 June, when he scorched to a four-ride paid maximum (11+1), as the Bristol boys ran riot to win 56-22. This was the beginning of a real purple patch at his home circuit, for the hard-riding American repeated that score in a Gulf British League match versus Coventry on 24 June, and when he did it for a third successive week against Leicester on 1 July, he appeared to be on the verge of greatness. However, after representing the Bulldogs in two further meetings, he had to return home for the World Championship qualifying rounds, causing him to miss eight league fixtures, plus two in the Knock-Out Cup, and a challenge match. While away, he did well enough to reach the American Final, held at Costa Mesa, California on 29 July, but with a total of 8 points in the big event, it meant he finished among the non-qualifiers for the next stage of the World Championship trail.

'Gresh' announced his return with a bang, when he netted a paid maximum (11+1) in a league encounter against Reading at Eastville on 12 August, before a mini-slump in form resulted in a batch of comparatively low scores. He bounced back to complete the month in style though, hitting another paid full-house (9+3) against visiting Hackney Wick. His performances generally remained good thereafter, especially when he rode unbeaten to notch 14+1 points versus Sheffield on 30 September. That was his fifth paid maximum of the league campaign, and his final figures revealed that Steve had totalled 168 points from 26 matches, yielding an average of 7.06 – but the Bristol management realized there was much more to him than pure statistics. One way or another, he was a crowd-pleaser, with his racing style often getting him into scrapes on the track, and he was also a media person's joy, because he was always doing something newsworthy.

The Californian again lined up for the Bulldogs in 1978, and did his utmost to make sure it would be a memorable year, plundering 286 points from 30 league matches, as his overall league average shot up to 9.24. His figure around Eastville was exactly 10.00, but whereas in the past Steve had tended to be steady, if unspectacular in his away scoring, he really came into his own to achieve an 8.39 return. Tall scores were a regular feature of home matches, the highlights being 12-point maximums against Leicester, Reading and Belle Vue in the league, with the latter two being recorded in a brilliant double-header display on 6 October. Meanwhile on his travels, there was 13 points at Leicester, 14 at Wolverhampton, 11 at Cradley Heath, 9+2 at Birmingham, 9+1 at Coventry, 9+1 at Swindon, and the list goes on and on. There was also one other away showing of real note in a Knock-Out Cup tie at Leicester on 6 June, when Steve simply blitzed through the card to register a five-ride maximum in a thrilling 39-39 draw.

On the individual front, he was seeded direct to the Inter-Continetal Final at Fredericia, Denmark on 2 July, when, despite two exclusions, he still notched 7 points and just missed out on a place in the World Final. Sadly, it was the closest he ever got to an appearance in the sport's biggest meeting.

With Bristol being forced to close down after the season's end, both Steve and Phil Crump subsequently joined forces with promoter Wally Mawdsley, when he took over at Swindon in 1979. The American, it appeared, would be the replacement for Swedish ace Jan Andersson, who had been transferred to Reading. Just how fans of the Robins would react to Steve the extrovert, replacing the quiet, yet very popular introvert, intrigued many a scribe, however, once installed in the team, the poacher became the game-keeper, as his all-round efforts quickly won over the Blunsdon faithful. He was to remain with the Wiltshire side for three years, during which time he netted 532 points from 83 league matches, his best season occurring in 1980, when he attained a 7.40 average.

Steve linked with Reading in 1982, and whilst he did his best for the Racers, a couple

of hefty knocks saw him struggle for fitness, and having recorded just 113 points from 23 matches, his league average dropped to 5.41.

Returning to Swindon in 1983, 'Gresh' rode superbly on a borrowed machine to record 11 points in his first meeting back, a League Cup encounter with Hackney Wick at Blunsdon on 26 March. Sadly, he never again showed that sort of form and his scoring drained away, with things reaching a head following a single point return from a Knock-Out Cup tie at Wimbledon on 30 June.

Steve subsequently returned to America to sort out what he described as 'personal problems', but that proved to be the end of his career, and he is remembered as a real character who could beat the very best on his day. That fact was recognized internationally during his latter years in Britain, as he represented the USA in four Test series against England (1980-83), playing a part in his country's overall successes of 1980 and 1982.

Competition	Matches	Points
League	22	119
National Trophy	2	6
ACU Cup	6	38
Challenge	7	48
Bulldogs Total	**37**	**211**

Although always known as Morian, speedway's real first 'Great Dane' was actually born Jens Henning Fisker Hansen on 10 January 1905, in Copenhagen. It seems, he always had a interest in 'things mechanical', and it was in 1928, that he was employed as a car tester at the Ford factory in his native land. Two years later, Morian came to ride on these shores, and appeared in an international meeting at Belle Vue, prior to joining Southern League West Ham the following term. He was to then miss a year of British activity, but again linked with the Custom House based side in 1933, when he netted 49 points from a dozen league matches, while also furthering his experience by touring England with a Danish team.

After remaining absent in 1934, the Dane resumed with Hackney Wick in 1935, and it was there that he really began to make a name for himself, scoring 74 league points for the club in what was their first season of racing.

Morian was again at the 'Wick' in 1936, when supporters of the Wolves, as they were then known, saw a very different rider to the one of the previous year. Before their eyes was a rider who sat upright in the saddle, and rode with a great deal of confidence. This was aptly reflected in the final statistics, which revealed a much-improved tally of 179 points in league racing. However, there can be no doubt that his major achievement was reaching the initial World Final at Wembley Stadium on 10 September, and by virtue of recording 48 points in the qualifying rounds, he carried 10 bonus points into the big event. Sadly, although he gave of his best, Morian finished well down the field with 5 points on the night, but at least he had qualified for the historic occasion.

In 1937, he was again a big scorer for Hackney Wick, plundering 182 points from a full quota of 24 National League matches as the Wolves finished fifth out of seven teams. With 45 points from the so-called preliminary and championship rounds, he made his second and last appearance in the World Final at Wembley on 2 September too. He fared a tad better on this occasion, his 8-point tally including a twelfth-heat victory over Bill Kitchen, Frank Varey and Tommy Croombs. Added to the 7 bonus points he took into the meeting, the Dane totalled 15 points (as he had done the year before), but again finished in the bottom half of the overall scorechart.

In 1938, Hackney Wick opted for a move down to the newly-created Division Two of the National League, so Morian was transferred to Bristol, together with team-mates Cordy Milne and Vic Duggan, the Bulldogs having been awarded top-flight status in place of the London side. His club debut subsequently occurred in a challenge match against New Cross at Knowle Stadium on 15 April, when the homesters were well beaten 62-43. However, Morian had a marvellous match, looking self-assured as he top-scored for his new team with 13 points. Bristol's first home league match took place against Harringay on 22 April, with the return encounter against the Tigers being staged at the Londoner's Green Lanes raceway the following day. A very happy set of Bulldogs raced to success in both fixtures, 47-36 at Knowle, and 42-41 at Harringay, with Morian enjoying two excellent meetings to net 10 points in each. Sad to relate though, these were the only times when he gleaned double-figures during the entire league campaign, although he did have a good night against Belle Vue on 19 August, when he ended up with 7+3 points to his name. Aside from that, his next best scores at home were 8+1 against both Wimbledon and West Ham, while on the team's travels, he managed 8 points at West Ham and Belle Vue. His end-of-year total of 119 points from 22 league matches represented a considerable slump in the form he had shown for Hackney Wick, with his main problem being a lack of consistency.

No one could ever be sure what this most likeable of chaps would come up with, and he, himself was the first to realize if he hadn't come up to scratch, as his boss Ronnie Greene confirmed on one occasion when he stated 'If he doesn't ride well, you don't have to tell him – he knows.' He also added 'Morian never makes excuses, he always says that it's all down to him.' The Dane had, however, proved to be an excellent team man who always had a cheery word for everyone, staff, fans and fellow riders alike. He was also as strong as an ox, and as tough as teak. One of his team-mates claimed he once saw Morian pick up his machine and just hurl it down, not in temper, but in sheer frustration. Unfortunately, Bristol finished bottom of the Division One table, having accumulated just 13 points, and it came as little surprise when they exchanged their licence with South-ampton in order to return to Division Two racing for the 1939 season. That meant a fond farewell to Morian, who went to Wembley, with Cordy Milne joining Southampton, and Vic Duggan linking with Wimbledon.

With Wembley, the popular Dane did reasonably well to notch 108 league points from 19 matches prior to the outbreak of war, his best performance being a paid maximum (9+3) in a home match against New Cross on 10 August. He also weighed in with three tremendous performances against South-ampton, with tallies of 10+1 and 8+3 at Wembley Stadium, plus a score of 9+1 at the Saints' Banister Court circuit.

When the Second World War broke out, he was enlisted in the Royal Air Force as a Flying Officer, and his courage later saw him decorated with the George Medal and the Distinguished Flying Cross. He spent many years living in retirement in his Danish homeland, and right up to his untimely death, was a member of the Veteran Speedway Riders' Association in this country. There can be no doubting Morian Hansen was an absolute 'one-off' – they simply don't make them like that anymore.

The programme from Morian Hansen's Bristol Debut, against New Cross on 15 April 1938.

Competition	Matches	Points
League	34	324
Knock-Out Cup	6	66
Inter-League KOC	2	17
Spring Gold Cup	5	42
Challenge	7	55
4 Team Tournament	4	30
Bulldogs Total	**58**	**534**

Phillip Edwin Herne was born in Ballina, New South Wales, Australia on 27 March 1955, and first came to the UK in 1973, when he joined Birmingham, who were then operating in the British League Division Two. Phil quickly showed he was a young man with a very bright future, since he settled down to notch 219 points from 33 league matches for a very satisfactory 7.52 average. He was also capped by Australasia in the Division Two Test series against England, scoring a total of 16 points from 3 matches as his side took victory by 2 matches to 1.

With a most satisfactory season under his belt, Phil returned to Birmingham for the 1974 season, and his form was nothing short of sensational. In accumulating 335 points from 31 league matches, he not only topped the Brummies averages on a sensational 10.78 figure, but was also the leading man in the entire league. Spearheaded by Phil, plus sterling efforts from Arthur Browning, John Hart and George Major, it was a terrific year for the West Midlands side as they completed a fabulous double, winning the League

Championship and Knock-Out Cup. Needless to say, Phil was red-hot favourite for the Division Two Riders' Championship at Wimbledon on 28 September, but on the night, having netted 12 points, he had to be satisfied with third spot behind Champion Carl Glover, and runner-up Ted Hubbard.

The brilliant Aussie had made odd top-flight appearances during his first two seasons of racing on these shores, and it was obvious he would move up on a full-time basis in 1975, when he linked with Newport in the renamed British League, joining forces with fellow countrymen Phil Crump and Neil Street. He duly took to top-league racing like a duck to water, scoring well wherever he rode, to finish the league campaign with a tally of 229 points from 29 matches.

Remaining with the Welsh club in 1976, Phil provided superb back-up to the mighty Phil Crump, gleaning 222 points from 26 league matches for a superb 9.77 average, and twelfth place in the overall Gulf British League figures. The year also saw a proud Phil Herne become a World Champion on 19 September, when he notched 7 points as Australia took victory ahead of Poland, Sweden and the Soviet Union in the World Team Cup final at London's White City Stadium.

In 1977, the Newport management transferred their operation to Bristol, and they naturally wanted the two Phil's to lead the new Bulldogs from the front. After making his debut with a 7 point return from their first league match at Wolverhampton on 1 April, the man from Ballina indeed did take care of the bulk of Bristol's scoring, along with 'Crumpie' of course. Despite the almost regular complaints about the Bristol circuit, Phil rode it as well as anyone, proving that a class rider can ride and score points whatever the conditions. League maximums were gleaned around the Eastville strip against Coventry (12), Leicester (11+1), Reading (12), Hull (12) and Swindon (15), while on his travels, he knocked up unbeaten totals at Leicester (12) and Birmingham (15).

The year wasn't completely smooth running, however, as he requested a transfer during the Bulldogs league match against Hackney Wick at Eastville on 30 August, after a disagreement over the constitution of the visitor line-up. This resulted in him being placed on the transfer list by the management, but after missing the following match at Exeter, he agreed to fulfil the remainder of his engagements for the club until the end of the season.

Indeed, his superb form steadied the Bristol ship, particularly after Phil Crump had broken a leg at Sheffield on 15 September. Looking at the statistics for 1977, Phil registered 324 points from 34 league matches for an average of 9.18, and when all meetings were taken into account, his total of points for the year rose to an amazing 534 for the Bulldogs!

For a reported fee of £7,000, he subsequently rejoined Birmingham, who had moved into speedway's top division two years previously. With 301 points from 35 matches, he finished on top of the Brummies league averages, having posted an 8.61 figure, his record for the season including a tremendous five-ride full-house at Reading on 24 March, plus a 12-point maximum at home to King's Lynn on 22 May.

Remaining with the West Midlanders in 1979, his scoring slipped to 227 points from 33 league fixtures for a reduced average of 7.47, but with the capacity to improve on that, he was unsurprisingly retained for the following season. Sadly, for both Phil and Birmingham, he suffered a hand injury, which was slow to heal, and he returned to Australia, having ridden in just 7 league matches for 27 points.

After requesting a transfer during the winter months, he was signed by Leicester promoter Martin Rogers. Phil worked hard to rediscover his old touch with the Lions, and it initially looked as if he was on the right road with a series of good scores in the League Cup competition. However, he was then hampered by a number of knocks, and although he never stopped trying, his British League scoring was restricted to 115 points from 25 matches as a result.

He was to line-up with the Blackbird Road outfit for a further two seasons, and after showing a slight improvement in 1982, his form seemed to desert him in 1983. It was then that Richard Vowles, who had taken over as Swindon promoter, stepped in to acquire the services of the experienced Aussie, as he saw him as the ideal man to stiffen-up the reserve berth of his struggling side. The judgement of the Robins' boss proved spot on, as the former Leicester man gave his old team-mate Phil Cump (who had almost been racing the opposition on his own), some useful backing to net 88 points from 22 league matches for a 5.38 average.

The short stint at Swindon brought the curtain down on Phil's career in Britain, but he is remembered here as a truly great Bristol rider, not only for his points plundering, but for his holding together of the side in 1977, when being a true professional, he didn't let a dispute stop him from doing his very best for the team, especially when they lost Phil Crump through injury.

Competition	Matches	Points
League	233	1,723
National Trophy	29	241
British Speedway Cup	13	66
Anniversary Cup	16	135
Spring Cup	6	41
Coronation Cup	16	102
Southern Shield	12	105
Challenge	77	629
4 Team Tournament	2	9
Mini-Matches	5	27
Bulldogs Total	**409**	**3,078**

In the proud history of Bristol Speedway, the date of 16 August 1946, is of particular importance, for it was on that day that a young man from Bath arrived at Knowle Stadium asking for a trial. Born on 23 October 1919, the person in question was one William Stanley Alfred Hole, and having been granted his wish, he made the most of it, winning the two races he participated in.

Billy was immediately offered a Bristol contract, and subsequently made his debut for the Bulldogs a week later on 23 August, when he failed to trouble the scorers in a challenge match against Sheffield. That was to prove the start of something big however, as Billy went on to give Bristol terrific service, remaining with the club right the way through until 1955, when the track was forced to close prematurely due to tumbling attendance figures. Indeed, he was appointed team captain when the Bulldogs were granted entry to Division Two of speedway's National

League in 1947, and it was a position he rightfully held until the aforementioned cessation of racing.

It may well have been due to his success with the club that later on his two younger brothers, Johnny and Graham, joined Bristol too. Referring back to the 1946 season, Billy was to end the open-licence campaign with 7 appearances and 24 points under his belt, his best showing being half-dozen returns against both Newcastle and Birmingham. When Bristol entered league racing in 1947, it understandably took them several weeks to find their feet, but after a few teething problems, they got their act together, becoming a more than useful outfit around their own Knowle Stadium strip. The Bulldogs were to end the year in sixth position out of eight teams, and Billy enjoyed a sound first full season to register a total of 166 points from the 28-match league programme. The season had barely begun, when Billy showed what an excellent prospect he was by racing to a four-ride maximum at Wigan. The match in question took place on 3 May, but his efforts weren't enough to save Bristol from a 49-35 defeat. What was all the more remarkable about his performance, however, was the fact that he had crashed in the previous evening's home match against Middlesbrough, and worked through the night with brother-in-law and fellow Bulldog Eric Salmon to repair his badly buckled bike!

In 1948, Bristol put into practice what they had learned on track the year before, blasting to the League Championship in fine style. Much of their success was due to an excellent team spirit and the inspired captaincy of Billy Hole who always led from the front. Full or paid maximum returns were a regular contribution to the Bristol cause from Billy, and to prove (if proof were necessary) that all circuits were alike to him, one only has to look at the beginning of October. The first day of the month saw the Bulldogs hammer Newcastle 67-17, and he lead the way with an unbeaten dozen points around the 290-yard raceway. Then, the following day, Bristol were in action at Norwich, a 425-yard track that was different in every way to the Knowle strip. It made no difference, however, as the Bulldogs surged to a 50-34 victory, with their skipper recording another faultless maximum. The end-of-term statistics revealed he had notched up 266 points, having remained ever-present throughout the league campaign for a second successive season.

After being forced to stay in Division Two, Bristol were to again dominate their sector of racing in 1949, securing the Championship by a 10-point margin from runners-up Sheffield. Billy had a truly outstanding season, racking up a massive 429 points as he again parti-cipated in each and every league match, but perhaps more importantly, he was the highest scorer in the entire division, finishing 30 points ahead of Cradley Heath's Alan Hunt. At home, he recorded no fewer than 14 full maximums, while on his travels, he went through the card on another 4 occasions. He also won the Division Two Match Race Championship, when defeating Ashfield's Ken Le Breton (the rider affectionately referred to as the 'White Ghost'), prior to losing the title to Phil Clarke of Norwich.

Bristol were finally promoted to the Division One in 1950, but as is well documented, they were given little assistance by 'the powers that be', although Billy took the higher sphere of racing in his stride to again head the side's scoring on 186 points. This was despite being forced to miss a few meetings in mid-season after having the misfortune to break a bone in his leg during a challenge match at Shelbourne on 23 July. The going was undeniably hard in top-flight racing, but it must be regarded as some kind of success that the Bulldogs at least managed to avoid the wooden spoon, finishing seventh in a league of nine teams.

Sadly, the 1951 season saw a big drop in crowds at Bristol, brought about by a crippling Entertainment Tax and the team's failure to really cut it amongst the elite. The best they could do was sixth position in the final table, but thankfully, Billy was still a quality act, scoring 199 points and remaining ever-present for the fourth time in five seasons. A personal highlight occurred on 16 June, when Swindon staged an individual meeting for the Silver Trophy, featuring all the Bristol rides, plus some leading lights from Division Two. Showing his class, Billy equalled the track record in the opening race, before establishing a new best time of 74.6 seconds for the 410-yard circuit in heat five. He went on to take the chequered flag in each of his other three rides, thereby securing an emphatic success with a superb 15-point maximum.

Billy tended to go off the boil a wee bit in 1952, nevertheless, he still totalled 149 points in the league, and was still a more than useful contributor around his home track. Unfortunately, it was another year of struggle for the Bulldogs in the top division, with the team finishing eighth out of the ten participants.

Worse was to follow in 1953, however, when their weaknesses were laid bare for all to see, and they slumped to the basement position in the final table. For Billy, it was a season to forget, as his scoring tailed-off, and he only managed to accumulate 75 league points.

Bristol chose to be 'demoted' back to Division Two in 1954, where running costs were considerably less, and they had a much more enjoyable time of it, emerging as League Champions once more. Billy enjoyed an improved season too, scoring 139 points and displayed a lot of his old fire and dash. It wasn't a particularly good year for the Bristol management though, for despite having a winning team, attendance figures could have been much better. The crowd levels were again cause for alarm in 1955, and things got so bad that Bristol were forced to close down after defeating Rayleigh 50-46 in a league encounter on 17 June. Billy was going well before the enforced closure and looked set for a very good season, having plundered 114 points from 13 league meetings. He subsequently accepted a posting to see out the year with Exeter, and used his experience to good effect, knocking up a total of 93 league points for the Falcons.

At the end of the campaign, he announced his retirement from active speedway – the sport he had served with distinction. Billy had been a marvellous servant to Bristol, and it is very likely that remaining loyal to such an 'unfashionable' club had cost him many England caps. He could have joined any top league club had he wished to, but was happy to just be a Bulldog, and a mighty fine one he was too.

Competition	Matches	Points
League	209	811
National Trophy	28	151
Provincial League KOC	4	42
Anniversary Cup	14	30
Spring Cup	6	21
Coronation Cup	16	55
Southern Shield	12	79
Western Cup	4	33
Challenge	69	276
4 Team Tournament	2	15
3 Team Tournament	1	3
Mini-Matches	7	39
Junior League	31	114
Bulldogs Total	**403**	**1,669**

John Derrick Hole was born in Bath, Somerset on 18 December 1924, and was the younger brother of long-time Bristol skipper Billy. He joined his local team in 1947 as a raw novice, and it was claimed that he built his first bike from odds and ends passed onto him by brother Billy, and brother-in-law Eric Salmon. Whether this was actually true isn't known, but Johnny was to make excellent progress during the second-half events, prior to claiming a team place at the beginning of following year.

His first-team debut subsequently occurred in a challenge match against a combined Southampton and Hastings side at Knowle Stadium on 19 March, when he marked the occasion with a point. With a style obviously modelled on his elder sibling, Johnny worked hard to improve his racing, and at the end of a year which saw Bristol crowned Division Two Champions, he had accumulated 53 points

from 26 league matches. It's fair to say he struggled on his travels, but at Knowle he was usually good for a useful tally, his best performance being against Sheffield on 14 May, when a 6-point return (from just 2 starts) included a fabulous heat-eight victory over Bruce Semmens. He also finished a couple of other home meetings with unbeaten two-ride scores of 5+1 against Glasgow on 24 September and Newcastle on 1 October.

As the history books tell us, Bristol went on to again land the Division Two title in 1949, and Johnny made excellent progress during the year. Evidence of this came with a score of 8+2 points at Glasgow, plus 7+1 at both Coventry and Walthamstow. At home, he was a regular contributor to the weekly thrashings meted out by the rampant Bulldogs, with 9 points against Southampton being his highest total on 26 August. Capping a fine year, he was part of the side that created history when beating Glasgow by the maximum possible score of 70-14 at Knowle on 7 October, his score on the night being an unbeaten 5+1 from two starts. The end of season facts and figures revealed just how much improvement he had made, for his total of 149 league points from 43 matches was an excellent effort by any standards.

Despite his limited experience, Johnny stayed put with the Bulldogs upon their elevation to Division One in 1950, giving the higher sphere of racing his best shot. In home matches, he did reasonably well, but it was a different story on the road, although he did manage to knock-up scores of 5 points in both of Bristol's visits to West Ham. It was generally a season of struggle for the team, but in saying that, they did do well to avoid the wooden spoon, finishing seventh in the final league table above Birmingham and basement side Harringay, with Johnny's contribution to the cause being 73 points from 30 matches.

The Bulldogs fared slightly better in 1951, moving a notch up the Division One standings to sixth spot, with Johnny showing a marginal increase in scoring to register 84 points, having remained ever-present throughout the 32 league fixtures.

Unfortunately, Bristol slumped back to eighth place in 1952, and it was obviously tough at the top for a club unfairly labelled with an 'unfashionable' tag. Thanks to a dislocated ankle, courtesy of striking Arthur Atkinson's rear wheel at Harringay on 27 June, Johnny only appeared in 18 of the side's 36 league matches, gathering a total of 70 points, with his best performances reserved very much for the Knowle faithful.

The downward trend continued for the Bulldogs the following year, when they ended the campaign occupying the cellar position. Despite this, Johnny enjoyed a better time of things, racing in all 16 matches of the shortened league programme for 86 points, his tally being sufficient for him to finish third in the team's scoring chart, behind Dick Bradley and Jack Unstead. Indeed, his efforts included one terrific night at Belle Vue on 18 July, when he scorched to 10 points from the no.8 berth – although he was unable to save Bristol from a 46-37 defeat.

Having applied to be 'relegated', the Bulldogs went on to take the Division Two league title by 4 clear points from a powerful Poole outfit in 1954. The move down benefited Johnny, for he put in his usual 100 per cent commitment to succeed where some of his colleagues failed, again remaining ever-present throughout the 20 league matches, and recording 108 points in the process. These were, however, difficult times for Bristol Speedway, with crowds dropping and stock car racing being the motor sport that attracted the local public.

Sadly, in June 1955, Knowle Stadium closed its doors to the two-wheeled variety of racing, and at the time of their demise, the Bulldogs had completed 14 league matches, of which Johnny had ridden in just half-a-dozen for a tally of 16 points. After taking a break, Johnny returned to the speedway scene for the start of 1956, when he joined former team-mate Dick Bradley at Southampton.

Over the next three years, his pleasing-on-the-eye style thrilled the regulars at Banister Court, as he garnered a total of 230 league points for the Saints during that time. Still with Southampton in 1959, his appearances were limited, although he was also to represent the Hampshire outfit in the National Reserve League. The year saw a mid-season revival of the sport at Johnny's first love Bristol, and he was only too pleased to again don the famous Bulldogs race-jacket in 3 of their open-licence meetings, scoring a total of 11 points.

During the winter months, important discussions took place at the highest level in speedway, with the result being the formation of a 10-team Provincial League in 1960. Johnny actually began the year with Southampton, but when Bristol were admitted to the new league, it came as no surprise when he was asked to skipper the reformed side, his vast experience, and the fact that he was a former teamster making his appointment a 'must'. Happily, ex-young Bulldogs Cliff Cox and Roy Taylor also returned to the fold, as did veteran Frank Evans, so there were a number of connections with the past for old-time supporters to identify with.

In what was his best-ever season in the sport, Johnny was an inspirational captain, leading the team from the front as he compiled 172 points from the 18-match league programme. Full maximums were recorded in home matches against Bradford, Stoke and Yarmouth, with Johnny also chalking up a four-ride full-house against the latter, when Bristol visited the Norfolk track on 28 June. Meanwhile, he also plundered paid maximums in the home (10+2) and away (11+1) encounters with Liverpool, plus the Knowle-staged fixture with Sheffield (11+1). His endeavours helped the side to third place in the league, only just behind Champions Rayleigh, and runners-up Poole. He also played no little part in Bristol's glorious Knock-Out Cup run, which culminated in a 100-89 aggregate success over Rayleigh in the final – his contribution including scores of 12+2 at Edinburgh in the semi-final, and 13+2 in the second leg of the final at Knowle.

There was no doubting his dedication to the Bulldogs and he played a big part in bringing speedway racing to a brand new set of enthusiasts, as well as the many old fans who returned to cheer on their heroes in orange and black. Johnny's efforts were certainly recognized in the *Speedway Star Digest* ratings for 1960, with him deservedly placed second behind team-mate Trevor Redmond, who had also done much to help Bristol with their achievements during the season. On 30 September, the Bulldogs management thanked the supporters, and looked forward to again seeing everyone at Easter in 1961. Sadly, that final meeting for the Bristol Cup was rained-off, but nevertheless, the fans had little doubt that their beloved Bulldogs would be back, with Johnny Hole leading the team.

Unfortunately, there was a big shock in store for the riders, management and sup-porters, when, on 23 January 1961, the *Bristol Evening Post* carried a headline story that Knowle Stadium had been sold for £130,000. That spelt the end of speedway, and Johnny subsequently retired from active racing, having made a wonderful contribution to the sport in the city.

Competition	Matches	Points
League	14	69
National Trophy	3	15
Provincial Trophy	1	0
English Speedway Trophy	5	15
Union Cup	2	9
Challenge	10	34
Mini-Matches	1	2
Bulldogs Total	**36**	**144**

Born in Wandsworth, London on 26 July 1913, Charles Ronald Howes went on to enjoy a long career in the saddle, throughout which, he preferred to be known by the shortened version of his middle name. His interest in speedway began when he initially watched the magical Vic Huxley in action, and the story goes that the Australian noticed the young Ron hanging around the Wimbledon pit area, and gave him a job cleaning his bike. Upon leaving school, he took a job as a mechanic, but it was always apparent he was far more interested in the riding side of the sport, and he began pleading for practice rides around the Plough Lane bowl. His wish was eventually granted, with him impressing sufficiently enough to break into the Dons side in 1934.

Unfortunately, Ron didn't get any league outings the following year, but again claimed a

team spot in 1936, and although the standard was high, he stuck at his task, remaining with the London outfit until dropping out of the side in July 1938. He was to spend the rest of the campaign in Division Two with Southampton, prior to remaining in the same sphere of racing with Bristol in 1939. This wasn't his first experience with the Bulldogs, however, as in 1936, he had been non-riding reserve in a challenge match against Plymouth on 10 July. Then, on 29 September 1937, he was drafted into the Bristol team for a 9-heat challenge match at Southampton, scoring 2 points in a 34-20 defeat. The Bulldogs won the Provincial League Championship that year, and after being granted promotion, subsequently endured a disastrous term in Division One. It was therefore no surprise when it was announced that the men in orange and black would be spending 1939 in Division Two.

Ron began the season quietly with 2 points in an away mini-match against Wimbledon Reserves, followed by a single point at Crystal Palace in an English Speedway Trophy encounter. His scoring was steady, if unspectacular thereafter in that competition, before he really scaled the heights in a National Trophy tie against Crystal Palace at Knowle on 16 May. The Bristol boys ran riot to provide the race winner of each and every heat, scoring 5-1s in no fewer than 14 races as they hammered their hapless opponents 83-22, with Ron's contribution being a super paid maximum of 10+2 points. As the league programme got underway, he rode hard for his points, and although they generally seemed hard to come by, he did produce several good performances, especially on the road. Fine examples of this occurred with tallies of 7+1 points at both Newcastle (3 July) and Hackney Wick (15 July), although his efforts couldn't prevent defeat in either match. Completing a wonderful month personally, he returned with the side to Newcastle on 24 July, when he notched a score of 8 points. Meanwhile, at Knowle, he recorded 6+1 points on three occasions against Norwich, Newcastle and Belle Vue Reserves, with his top score being 6+2 versus Sheffield. The latter match, incidentally, took place on 25 August, and was the final meeting at Knowle Stadium before the Second World War brought everything to a standstill. With all matches against Crystal Palace and Middlesbrough expunged from official records due to the earlier closure of both venues, Ron's record for his stint with the Bulldogs showed 69 points, having ridden in all 14 league matches completed by the club prior to the halt.

When league speedway started-up again in 1946, he linked with West Ham to register 36 points from 16 matches, while also finding time to again represent Bristol (who were running with an open licence), in 8 challenge fixtures for 32 points. The following year, Ron was associated with Wimbledon, but opportunities were scarce, and in fact, he only made 3 league appearances, gleaning but a single point.

He stayed with the Dons in 1948, but was frustratingly restricted to just 2 league matches, and an equal number of points. Thankfully though, Rayleigh had begun staging the 'shale game' on an open licence, with general manager Frank Arnold happy to appoint Ron as team skipper for their series of challenge matches. It was natural then, that when the Rockets joined Division Three a year later, they would retain the services of the Londoner, having paid out a £100 transfer fee. Having handed over the captaincy to Pat Clarke, Rayleigh only just avoided the basement position in their first season of league activity,

that unwanted 'honour' instead going to Oxford, but Ron enjoyed a fairly productive time of it, recording 181 league points.

In 1950, the Rockets again finished just one position off the bottom of the table, although the man from Wandsworth remained unruffled to accumulate 219 points. He was to remain with Rayleigh until retirement beckoned in 1954, during which time he helped them to Southern League Championship glory on two occasions (1952 and 1953), and took his total of league points for the club to 745½.

Ron had one other claim to fame, which happened during the filming of the movie *Once a Jolly Swagman* (released in 1948) starring Dirk Bogarde, when he was used as the 'stand in' for the action scenes.

Although interrupted by the war, few riders' careers have spanned so many summers as that of Ron's, and he was honoured in 1988, when the Veteran Speedway Riders' Association elected him their President for the year.

Sadly, during the final preparation of this book, the authors learned of the death of Ron at the age of nearly ninety, in July 2003.

Competition	Matches	Points
League	17	67
Knock-Out Cup	2	3
Inter-League KOC	2	4
Spring Gold Cup	1	6
Challenge	3	10
Bulldogs Total	**25**	**90**

Hendrikus Constantinus Jozef Kroeze, to give him his full name, was born in Zenderen, Holland on 11 March 1952, and subsequently began riding in his homeland in 1971, prior to arriving in the UK to ride for Halifax three years later. He had certainly been prepared to travel around in order to further his speedway education, and had ridden in several countries, including Czechoslovakia, Denmark, Germany, Poland and Yugoslavia, so he was clearly a speedster of considerable experience when he arrived at the Shay.

The banked 400-yard Yorkshire circuit seemed ideal for the Dutchman, and he was to enjoy an excellent first season amid the cut and thrust of the British League Division One. The end-of-term statistics revealed he had participated in 29 league matches, and scored 147 points for a highly creditable 5.56 average, which by anyone's standards represented a fine start to racing in this country. To cap the year, Henny also completed a hat trick of victories in the Dutch National Championship, having previously captured the title in 1971 and 1972.

Everyone connected with Halifax hoped they would see big strides from him in 1975, but as is so often the case, it didn't pan out that way, and the man from Zenderen ended the campaign with a slightly reduced average of 5.17, having netted 119 league points. He did, however, manage to retain the Dutch National Championship, and enjoyed international honours when representing his country in both the World Team Cup and World Pairs.

Remaining with Halifax in 1976, Henny really came into his own, with an early indication of great things being a tally of 15+4 points in a Knock-Out Cup tie against Leicester at the Shay on 27 March. Several double-figure returns followed in the Northern Trophy, but he was then sidelined through injury for a spell in late May and early June. Having returned to the saddle, his confidence gradually returned, and a real high spot occurred when White City visited the West Yorkshire venue on 31 July. The London outfit left with the league points, having won a thriller of a meeting 40-38, but the talking point amongst the Dukes supporters was the breathtaking 20 points recorded by one Henny Kroeze on the night. As if to prove that was no fluke, the 'Flying Dutchman' went one better on 21 August, when he became the first British League rider to register a 21-point maximum in a 51-27 success over Birmingham in another league encounter at the Shay. Although he didn't scale those heights again, some other good scores followed, before his season was brought to a premature close when he suffered a broken thumb in a challenge match at Sheffield on 9 October. Needless to say, his final league figures for the year showed a huge improvement, with 241 points being gleaned from 26 matches for an average of 7.50.

Still with Halifax in 1977, Henny began the campaign well: a series of fine performances including four-ride maximums in home league matches against Hackney Wick and Hull. However, disaster struck in the Continental Final of the World Championship at Togliati, Soviet Union on 25 June, when he broke a thigh. Although he hoped to get back on track, his recovery proved long and he just couldn't make it. He had ridden in just 11 league matches for the Dukes, scoring 91 points for an average of 7.37, and in an end of season move he was transferred to Hull in a rider-exchange transaction involving Mitch Graham.

In the event, Henny didn't turn a wheel for the Vikings, as he was subsequently snapped up by Bristol, eventually making a late start to 1978, when first sporting the Bulldogs bib at Eastville in a league match against Wimbledon on 5 May. In what was an inauspicious start for the Dutchman, he notched just a single point, with Bristol sliding to a 41-37 defeat before an audience of 7,880. Unfortunately, an ankle injury, combined with the after-effects of his broken leg from the previous year, meant he was to be in and out of the team, and aside from notching 10 points at Sheffield on 15 June, fans of the Bulldogs never really saw him at his best until late-on in the season. At Eastville, scores of 7+1 against Ipswich, and a three-ride tally of 6+3 against Leicester

showed his true ability, and he followed up with a brilliant 13+2 return from an away match at Belle Vue on 30 September. To complete the year, he carded 5+2 points against Belle Vue, and 8+2 versus Exeter in home league matches, whilst in between hitting 8+1 from three starts in a challenge match against the Ole Olsen Select. In the final analysis, his record for the West Country club was 67 points from 17 league matches for an average of 5.35, which, considering he was based at a new venue, and was coming back from an awful injury, wasn't bad at all really.

With Bristol closing down, Henny had to find another team for 1979, and he returned to Yorkshire to link with Sheffield. Bad luck was to dog him again though, when he broke an ankle during practice for the World Pairs semi-final at Landshut, West Germany on 9 June. He missed a huge chunk of the year, and finished with only 12 league appearances under his belt for the Tigers, from which he averaged 5.40, having gleaned 46 points.

It is sad to relate that misfortune again held the upper hand in 1980, when he took several knocks, and missed numerous matches for Sheffield. The points proved hard to gather when he did ride, and after a series of poor performances, he returned to Holland in early September, bringing his British career to a close.

Little was heard of Henny for a few years, but in 1983, he was non-riding reserve at the World Final, so famously won by speedy West German Egon Muller in his homeland at Norden. Then in 1987, when the World Final was staged over two days at the Olympic Stadium in Amsterdam, Holland, Henny was nominated as his country's representative. However, it was not an occasion he would remember with much satisfaction, since he could only muster a single point, although a fall in his opening heat and a series of motor failures clearly didn't help his cause.

Competition	Matches	Points
League	26	48
National Trophy	1	1
Provincial Trophy	6	6
Coronation Cup	2	8
English Speedway Trophy	5	$19\frac{1}{2}$
Challenge	8	41
Bulldogs Total	**48**	**$123\frac{1}{2}$**

Reginald Edward Lambourne was born in Worcester on 1 July 1911, and like many speedway riders his career began on the grass-track scene. He subsequently joined Bristol Speedway in 1937, scoring 2 points on his debut against Liverpool in a league encounter at Knowle Stadium on 7 May. At the time, the Bulldogs were members of the Provincial League, and used many riders as they sought a winning combination, with Reg's limited outings mainly being from the reserve berth.

Come the end of the season, the efforts of the Bristol management bore fruit, with the side securing the league title ahead of Southampton. Despite suffering a shoulder injury and concussion when Nottingham rider Billy Lamont fell in front of him at Knowle on

28 May, Reg played his part in that success, netting a total of 29 points from 11 appearances. Whilst naturally, he found the going tough, he stuck at the job in hand to pick up several useful returns, including 5+1 tallies in home matches against both Birmingham and Norwich.

Following their glorious campaign, the Speedway Control Board decided to promote the Bulldogs to the National League Division One in 1938, and as well as again representing the West Country outfit, Reg also had rides for New Cross Reserves in the English Speedway Trophy. Bristol's elevation certainly didn't do Reg any favours, as he had only been racing seriously for a year, and here he was amongst the elite of the top-flight. In many ways, it meant beginning again, and points gathering was to prove extremely difficult. He was to muster a total of just 17 from 14 league fixtures. His highest return was 3+1 points, and this was achieved in the Bulldogs final match of season at Wembley on 6 October. In the event, it was an unhappy season for the club in the higher sphere of racing as they ended up with the wooden spoon, and it came as no surprise when they returned to Division Two in 1939.

Despite running in the lower league, team opportunities were limited, with Reg appearing in just two matches for a total of 3 points. To compound matters, one of these matches was an away encounter against Middlesbrough, and with the Teesside club resigning from the league in June, Reg's record for the season was therefore amended to 2 points, courtesy of one home fixture against Newcastle at Knowle on 7 July! He did, however, fare a little better in the English Speedway Trophy, accumulating 19½ points from 5 matches, his best performance occurring in the opening home fixture of the season against Crystal Palace on 25 April, when he garnered 7+1 points.

Due to the outbreak of war, the season was brought to a premature close at the end of August that year, and it wasn't until July 1946, that the roar of the bikes was again heard at Knowle Stadium when a series of open-licence meetings began with a view to a resumption of league activity in 1947. In the meantime, Reg had linked with Sheffield in the Northern League, although he did return to again race for the Bulldogs in 4 of their matches, accruing 25 points, including a superb tally of 10+2 against visiting Norwich on 6 September.

Although Bristol returned to league action in 1947, their fans didn't see Reg sporting the famous orange and black colours, as he linked with the newly-opened Wigan at their Poolstock Stadium home. He was to enjoy a good year in Division Two racing with the Warriors too, recording 144 points to finish third in the club's league scoring behind Dick Geary and Jack Gordon.

Having begun the 1948 season with 4 away league matches, the Wigan team subsequently transferred to Fleetwood, with Reg remaining on board to total 119 points. He was still with the Flyers at the beginning of 1949, until leaving in good time to link with Swindon for their grand opening challenge match against Oxford at Blunsdon on 23 July. Reg was to create his own little piece of history with the Robins, when, given his experience, he was appointed as the side's first captain. His brief was to help establish speedway racing in Swindon and during his five-season span with

the club, he certainly played a full part in achieving this. Briefly referring back to the unforgettable occasion of the Robins first meeting versus Oxford, Reg had quite a good club debut, scoring 7+1 points despite being a tad rusty, having not raced for a few weeks. When Hull were forced to close due to poor attendances, the Robins were on hand to take over their Division Three fixtures, and Reg was to appear in each of the short run of 13 league matches, netting 44 points for a 4.24 average.

In 1950, Reg gave a fine example of his sportsmanship and readiness to do anything to help Swindon's cause by handing over the captaincy to Mick Mitchell. As the season progressed, he displayed steady form, sometimes in the main body of the team and other times at reserve, but wherever he rode he always gave of his best, and by the end of the campaign he had notched up 143 points, giving him an improved league average of 6.09.

Early in 1951, Reg suffered a broken collarbone, and duly returned to the Swindon line-up following a time on the sidelines, only to end up appearing in second-half events after a dramatic loss of form. Typical of the man, he fought his way back into the side, with a late surge of form boosting his total of league points for the season to 103, giving him an almost identical average to the previous year of 6.10. Another loss of form was responsible for Reg again losing his team spot soon after the 1952 season had started, but as had happened before, it spurred him onto greater things and he had soon reclaimed his position. Despite riding many of his meetings from the reserve berth, he still improved his average to 6.32, having gleaned 138½ league points.

Reg was in the twilight of his career as the tapes went up on 1953, and he was restricted mostly to second-half rides, although he did go on to make eight league appearances, before calling it quits following an away match at Southampton on 7 July.

Tormod Langli

Competition	Matches	Points
League	68	456
Knock-Out Cup	6	39
Inter-League KOC	5	32
Spring Gold Cup	12	73
Challenge	12	68
4 Team Tournament	8	35
Bulldogs Total	111	703

Tormod Langli was born in Porsgrunn, Norway on 25 June 1952, and was a member of a speedway family, since his brother Hilge rode here in the United Kingdom, having short spells with both Newcastle in 1969, and Oxford in 1975.

Tormod's British career subsequently began with Newport in 1976, and he first rode for the club in a Gulf British League fixture at Hackney Wick on 19 March, when he netted just a single point. In the early matches of the season, he had to work hard for his points, although he did show excellent form against the Polish touring side on 6 April, when carding a paid maximum (8+4 points), as Newport went on the rampage to slaughter their visitors by 60 points to 17. Then, on 30 April, in a Spring Gold Cup match at the Welsh side's Somerton Park home, Tormod scored 9+1 points against Poole. It was these sort of performances that convinced the Newport management they had a real winner on their hands. He continued to make steady,

if unspectacular progress once the league campaign began, but his season was to unfortunately end abruptly on 29 August, when he broke a collarbone at Wolverhampton.

With his first year of British racing curtailed so cruelly, he had ridden in 24 matches, scoring 95 points for a very promising league average of 4.85. There was a great deal of activity during the winter months, with the Newport promoters moving their top-flight operation to Bristol, while the Welsh outfit entered a new team in the National League.

Happily, a fully recovered Tormod joined forces with former Newport team-mates Phil Crump, Phil Herne and Steve Gresham at the Eastville Stadium home of the reformed Bulldogs, where he quickly became the heart-throb of the female supporters. His debut for the side took place in a league encounter at Wolverhampton on 1 April, when, in a match to forget, he failed to score from 4 starts as Bristol suffered a 47-31 defeat.

Gradually, the Norwegian settled down, and as the season wore on, he became quite a force around the tricky 390-metre Eastville circuit. While the track was the cause of many moans from visiting riders, Tormod showed that it could be mastered, with some thought and application. He didn't manage to record any maximums, but a string of double-figure

returns flowed from his wheels in the cut and thrust of league activity, the best of which were 14 points against Hackney Wick on 30 August, and 13+1 versus White City on 14 October. It wasn't quite the same story away from home, however, but he did enjoy a particularly good night at Hull on 13 July, when he carded 11+2 points from 6 starts. At the end of a truly memorable season, when the Bulldogs had played to huge crowds, sometimes in excess of 10,000, Tormod had recorded a total of 210 league points from 34 fixtures for an average of 6.24. That really doesn't give a true reflection of his home form though, for 150 of those points were gleaned at Eastville, giving an average of 8.52.

When 1978 came along, he went better still around his home track, and more importantly, his scoring also improved on the road as he comfortably settled into a third heat-leader berth. Bristol started the campaign with a league match at Halifax on 18 March, and Tormod obliged with a tally of 9+1 points. Although the Bulldogs lost the match 44-34, the young Norwegian took the battle to the homesters, and his performance clearly set the tone for the season. On 26 May, Bristol beat Wolverhampton 44-33 in a league encounter at Eastville, and the significance of the meeting was a first paid maximum (11+1) for Tormod. Three days later, he hit 9+1 in an away match at Exeter, and a series of high scores were to follow, including a four-ride full-house against a British League Select in a challenge match on 9 June. As the year drew to a close, he recorded a couple more paid maximums on his home strip against Reading (10+2) in the league on 6 October, and versus the Ole Olsen Select (11+1) in a challenge match the following week.

In what was undoubtedly a great season for Tormod, perhaps his best showing occurred at Eastville on 19 May, when, having scored a dozen points, he filled the runner-up position behind Joe Owen in the Sunday Mirror World Championship/Volkswagen Grand Prix qualifying round. The meeting featured a field of very good riders, including his Bristol team-mates Phil Crump and Steve Gresham, plus the likes of Reg Wilson, Chris Morton and Michael Lee, so this represented a top-notch performance.

Sadly, there was to be no long-term future for the sport at Eastville, and on 18 December, it was formally announced that 'The Stadium Company had agreed not to hold, or permit to hold in the future, motorcycle speedway at the stadium.' This meant the break-up of the team, with all the riders moving on to pastures new.

It is worthwhile, however, to look at Tormod's final figures for 1978, which were impressive to say the least. At home, he plundered 160 points for an increased 9.51 league average, while with the addition of away matches, he totalled 246 points from 34 matches to produce a solid overall average of 7.32. These figures showed that he was a match for anyone in the Gulf British League at Eastville, yet he received precious little recognition from his country when it came to selecting riders for World Championship events. Quite why that should have been the case remains an unsolved mystery to this day.

In 1979, a cheque, said to be for £7,000 from Halifax, secured Tormod's services for the Dukes, and he made his club debut on 30 March, recording 8 points in a Northern Trophy match at Hull. He was to prove a consistent scorer around his Shay home, although not as dominating as he had been for Bristol, but he did manage to upgrade his away scoring. Come the end of his first term with the Dukes, he had garnered 191 points from 31 league matches for an average of 6.90.

Continuing with the Yorkshire side in 1980, Tormod rode in just three Northern Trophy matches, and one league fixture, before suffering a broken arm in a hang-gliding accident on Easter Monday. He tried a comeback later on in the season, only for misfortune to strike when he again broke his arm whilst practising in his native Norway. He subsequently asked for a transfer from Halifax, but no other club came forward, and Tormod was unfortunately lost to speedway in this country.

Competition	Matches	Points
League	27	152
National Trophy	4	21
Provincial Trophy	18	113
Coronation Cup	3	$16\frac{1}{2}$
Challenge	16	$86\frac{1}{2}$
Mini-Matches	1	2
Bulldogs Total	**69**	**391**

Cambridge born Frederick Leavis joined Bristol in 1936, upon the re-introduction of speedway to Knowle Stadium. Under the management of Ronnie Greene, the club were embarking on their first season of team speedway; the sport having previously been staged at the circuit between 1928-30, when the pioneer style of handicap and scratch racing was held.

Prior to linking with the West Country outfit, Fred had led something of a 'double life' in 1932, when he not only rode conventionally for Wimbledon, but also appeared under the pseudonym of Arthur Reynolds at grass speedway venues in Norfolk. He was actually elected captain of a Norwich side, which raced home matches at the original Firs Stadium site, against Staines, Lea Bridge and Celtic, as well as a couple of away fixtures at Yarmouth. The reason for his appearing under such a guise was that these circuits were not licensed and any rider spotted racing on them faced a fine or even suspension. However, where there's a will, there's a way, and our man from Cambridge wasn't the only one who devised a scheme to get around the strict regulations. He again rode at the Norwich venue in 1933, when he twice skippered a side called 'The Rest' against the homesters – however, on these occasions he used his real name!

Reverting back to his career in conventional speedway, Fred represented Wimble-

don for three seasons in all, before joining New Cross for the 1935 term, and he was also to race for the Old Kent Road side during his first season of activity with Bristol in 1936. Fred clearly liked using alternative names, as prior to first representing the West Country side, he rode under the pseudonym of Sonny Seymore in a grass-track meeting at the Old Rectory Grounds in Chipstream on 8 April. The event was held in aid of the Redhill Hospital, Surrey, and it proved a successful day for Mr Seymore as he won the Vic Huxley Cup.

Fred wasn't in the Bristol side for their historic first match at Nottingham on 28 April, but he was on board when the Knowle turnstiles clicked into gear for the first home meeting. That occurred on 8 May, when Southampton provided the opposition for a Provincial League fixture, with Fred netting 5+2 points in a hard-fought 38-32 success. In the next two home league matches, he managed to show impressive form, scoring 6+4 points against Cardiff, and a tally of 8 versus Liverpool, but despite this great start, his scoring was inclined to be inconsistent, especially on the team's travels.

There were some particularly outstanding nights though, when he revealed just how capable a rider he was. A prime example of this happened at Knowle on 31 July, when the Bristol boys trounced Liverpool 52-19 in a league encounter, with Fred joining in the points spree by rocketing to a fabulous four-ride maximum. Another fine example of how good he could be occurred on 18 September, when Plymouth arrived at the then nicknamed Bulldogs' home on league business, and were dispatched 49-23, with Fred notching a well taken 10 points. At the end of the campaign, Bristol occupied second spot in the final league table, and with Fred accumulating 68 points from 14 matches, he had clearly done sufficiently well to warrant a return in 1937.

The Bulldogs duly started their second season with a challenge match against New Cross at Knowle on 26 March, and in an encouraging performance they gained a 46-35 win, with Fred carding 6+1 points. The following week saw the staging of a Best Pairs event at the Bristol raceway, and on a very happy night for Fred and his dependable partner Harry Shepherd, they left the stadium as winners, having accrued 18 points between them. The success seemed to inspire him, as seven days later he romped to a classic 12-point maximum in a challenge fixture versus West Ham Reserves. He wasn't able to maintain that kind of high-scoring form on a regular basis, but there was always a good deal of effort, and several match-winning performances along the way. He did especially well when Liverpool provided the league opposition at Knowle, netting a paid maximum (11+1) on 7 May, and a four-ride full-house against the Merseysiders on 9 July. There were also significant contributions away at Birmingham (9+2) on 14 July, and against visiting Southampton (9) on 20 August. On top of those showings, Fred

recorded home and away tallies of 9+3 (paid maximum) and 10+1 respectively in Bristol's matches against Leicester, but these were sadly expunged from the records when the Midlanders withdrew from the league after completing just six fixtures. One other match in which Fred really shone was a Provincial Trophy encounter with Nottingham at Knowle on 2 July, when he carded an unbeaten tally of 14+4 points from six starts in a 60-47 victory. A look at the final statistics for the year revealed a total of 84 points from 13 league matches, which represented a noteworthy improvement on the previous term. While he quietly assumed the role of valuable back-up man to the heat-leaders, the Bulldogs put together a marvellous set of results, taking victory in 15 of their 20 matches, to win the League Championship by four clear points from 1936 Champions, Southampton.

With Bristol subsequently promoted to Division One in 1938, Fred went back to Wimbledon; but he had to wait until late August before claiming a team place, and only 8 league appearances followed for a meagre total of 8 points. Remaining with Wimbledon in 1939, it was even more difficult for him to break into the side, and he only ended up riding in 7 league matches, scoring but 4 points, prior to the outbreak of war.

Sadly, the hostilities brought his career to an end, but there can be no doubting he was well capable of filling a heat-leader role at Division Two level, had he been given the opportunity.

Finally, and rather interestingly, the authors have a letter to hand, which suggests Fred courted controversy during his time with the London side. The message, on Wimbledon Speedway Ltd notepaper, was signed by Dons promoter Ronnie Greene on 25 May 1938, and curtly headed 'Dear Leavis'. The rest of the letter was brief and to the point, stating 'Would you be good enough to let me know by return, why you did not accept the booking to ride at Wimbledon last Monday. Yours truly, Ronald W. Greene'.

Competition	Matches	Points
League	14	53
National Trophy	4	19
English Speedway Trophy	5	21
Union Cup	2	7
Bulldogs Total	**25**	**100**

Norman John Lindsay was born on 9 April 1917, in Melbourne, Australia, and began speedway racing early in 1939, making sufficient progress to consider a stint in the United Kingdom. It so happened that American ace Jack Milne had been touring Australia, and when he left in order to return to these shores in the continuance of his career with New Cross, Norman tagged along and travelled over with him.

Bristol, who had dropped back into Division Two following a disastrous campaign in the top-flight, had been on the look out for promising talent and were quick to snap up the young Aussie. His debut subsequently took place in an English Speedway Trophy match against Crystal Palace at Knowle on 25 April, when he made an inauspicious start by suffering a second heat fall. However, he recovered well to win his first race in Britain, when defeating team-mate Roy Dook and visitor Alf Markham later on in heat eleven. His final tally for the meeting was 5 points as Bristol claimed a 51-32 success in front of some 7,000 enthusiastic supporters.

Three days later, the Bulldogs journeyed to Middlesbrough for their first league match of the campaign, and received quite a hammering from the home side, losing 64-20. Despite being on the end of such a pasting, Norman rode as well as any of his colleagues to net 4 points, the same tally as both Jack Bibby and Ron Howes, with only Roy Dook bettering their totals on a single point more. On 9 May, Bristol entertained Norwich in the English Speedway Trophy, and although they

went down to a 43½-40½ defeat, Norman had every reason to be pleased with his personal contribution of 7 points, as only Jeff Lloyd scored more (8) for the men in orange and black. At the time, it was his best score since arriving in Britain and it showed, in case anyone doubted it, that he was a fighter and would surely continue to improve as the season progressed. As if to emphasize this, a week later he netted 8+1 points as Bristol ran riot to thrash Crystal Palace 83-22 in a National Trophy tie.

The league programme then continued in earnest, and when the Bulldogs visited Crystal Palace on 17 June, Norman registered 8+1 points as his side grabbed a 46-37 victory. Sadly, when all the end of term facts and figures were put together this figure was not included, since the London outfit withdrew from the league prematurely, as did Middlesbrough, and their records were expunged. The Australian had carded 6+1 points at home against Middlesbrough, plus the 4 points as previously mentioned when Bristol visited Teesside, so his overall record was considerably affected as a result. In addition, the Bulldogs lost the 2 league points they had gained over the North Easterners on 13 June, when they had narrowly won 43-41.

One other meeting of note occurred when Knowle Stadium played host to a Test match between England and the Dominions on 14 July. Norman was capped by the Dominions, and although he failed to score from two reserve outings, his team raced to a 63-44 victory, inspired by 18-point maximums from Eric Collins and Eric Chitty. On the domestic scene, Norman held his place in the Bristol side on merit, and when the outbreak of war brought a sudden end to the 'cinder game', he had recorded 53 league points from 14 matches. He had also gained much experience, and his gamble in coming to the UK was more than justified.

When war was declared, he remained on these shores until 1940, serving as a member of the Fire Service. He then returned to his homeland, and after joining the Australian Air Force, he saw service as a dispatch rider in New Guinea.

When the hostilities finally ceased, Norman waited until 1947, before returning to Britain to race for Harringay in the cut and thrust of Division One racing. The going was tough, however, and after registering 28 points from 11 league matches, he was transferred, along with Bernard 'Bat' Byrnes, to Division Two outfit Glasgow, in a deal that saw the London club acquire the services of Wal Morton. It was with the Scottish outfit that he found some consistent form to notch 90½ league points, and although the Tigers finished with the woodn spoon, better times were on the horizon.

Norman was to remain with Glasgow for a further four full seasons, during which time he gave them excellent service. In 1948 he hit 150 points in league racing, with that figure impressively rising to 218 the following season as he occupied fourth spot in the team's scoring behind Junior Bainbridge, Gordon McGregor and Will Lowther.

Back in his native land, Norman was capped by Australia in a Test match against England at Melbourne on 11 February 1950, netting 4 points as his side suffered a 58-50 loss.

Having returned to Scotland, he then accumulated 164 points from a shortened league programme as Glasgow shot up to the runner-up position in the Division Two table behind Norwich, thanks largely to the efforts of the sensational Tommy Miller who burst onto the scene with 251 points in his very first season of racing.

The Tigers fell back to tenth place in 1951, a year which saw Norman tally 145 points, thereby taking his total league haul for the Scottish side to 767½ points. That brought the curtain down on his British career, but in retirement, Norman couldn't be parted from motorbikes, since he subsequently used his leisure time for scrambles and trials riding.

Competition	Matches	Points
League	13	83½
National Trophy	4	39
Provincial Trophy	1	3
English Speedway Trophy	4	20
Union Cup	2	20
Challenge	8	107
Mini-Matches	1	0
Bulldogs Total	**33**	**272½**

Alfred Jeffrey Lloyd was born in Birmingham, West Midlands on 29 July 1914, and always preferred to be known by the shortened version of his middle name. He was a member of a well-known speedway family, since elder brother Wally also enjoyed much success, firstly as a rider and then as a manager. Having decided to follow his sibling into the sport, Jeff initially learnt the business as a Wembley Cub in 1936, prior to representing the famous London side's reserve team two years later in the English Speedway Trophy. Later that same year, he also made his Second Division debut with his hometown club Birmingham (Hall Green), making 7 league appearances for 26 points.

In 1939, a change of scenery saw him link with Bristol, where he was to prove both a useful scorer and popular crowd-pleaser. The opening action of the season saw four of the Bulldogs travel to Wimbledon for a mini-match, which was staged as a second-half attraction following a full-scale challenge meeting between the Dons and a combined New Cross/Norwich side on 7 April. The two-heat match resulted in a 7-5 win for the homesters, and it wasn't a beginning Jeff could look back on with much joy since he failed to score. There again, he only got the one programmed ride, so perhaps it wasn't too bad

after all! His first full match for Bristol subsequently occurred at Crystal Palace in the English Speedway Trophy on 22 April, but although his team were victorious by 46 points to 33, Jeff again remained point-less. He was to miss the next three matches, but upon his return to the Bulldogs line-up for an English Speedway Trophy match at Hackney Wick on 6 May, he looked a different rider in netting an 8 point tally, and topping the pile for his side. The scores began to flow thereafter, and when the men in orange and black really went to town to hammer Crystal Palace 83-22 in a National Trophy tie at Knowle Stadium on 16 May, Jeff chipped in with a brilliant paid maximum of 16+2 points.

In the league, he was always good for at least 5 points on his home circuit, with his most notable performances being 10+1 points against Hackney Wick, and totals of 9½ plus 1 bonus versus Norwich, and 9+1 when Belle Vue Reserves provided the opposition. As well as those great showings, he compiled 10+1 points against visiting Middlesbrough on 13 June, but with the Teesside club closing down shortly afterwards, this tally wasn't included in the season's records.

Meanwhile, on the road, he knocked-up 10+1 points at Crystal Palace on 17 June, although that was also later scrubbed from the year's statistics upon the Londoners withdrawal from the league not long after. He did go one race point better in an away match at Hackney Wick on 19 August, however, when he accumulated a tally of 11 in a 51-33 defeat, albeit in the Union Cup. With the season finishing early due to the outbreak of war, a glance at the facts and figures revealed a total of 83½ points from the 13 league matches that counted in Jeff's records, with only Harry Shepherd gleaning more for the Bulldogs.

During the war, he saw service in the RAF, and when regular speedway resumed in 1946 he joined Northern League Newcastle, recording a season's tally of 176 points to head the Diamonds scorechart. Remarkably, he made it through to the prestigious British Riders' Championship final, a competition which had been brought in as a temporary replacement for the World Final, while speedway re-established itself after the hostilities. Jeff's qualification for this was a fine achievement in itself as he had effectively qualified as a Division Two rider, although on the big night he could only muster 4 points.

The year also found him assisting at Bristol, who were operating on an open licence, with a view to joining the league the following year. His scores emphasized what a great rider he had become, for in just 7 matches back in the Bulldogs colours, he plundered 104 points, including an 18 point full-house against Middlesbrough on 16 August. On top of that, he also gained paid maximums of 12+3 against Norwich on 6 September, and 17+1 versus Sheffield on 18 October.

Jeff again lined-up at Newcastle in 1947, but after scoring 93½ league points, he moved into Division One racing with New Cross for a reputed £1,000 fee, with young Australian Ken Le Breton also going to the Geordie outfit as part of the deal. It was to prove money well spent by the Rangers, as the Birmingham-born racer went on to net 93 points from 14 league matches between June and the season's close.

In 1948, he remained ever-present throughout the 24-match league programme for New Cross, racking up 170 points for a solid 8.17 average, while also making his second appearance in the British Riders' Championship final, when he gleaned 5 points. With the league programme extended, Jeff again rode in the Rangers full quota of 42 matches in 1949, registering 275 points for a slightly reduced 7.31 average.

Having ridden 18 league matches for 105 points in 1950, New Cross took the unusual decision of letting him go to Harringay in an effort to 'equalize team strengths' as they put it at the time. They did, however, receive a reported £1,750 for his services from the Racers, which aside from all the points he had scored, also represented a tidy profit on the deal that originally brought him from Newcastle. Anyway, he was soon in the scoring groove for his new club, and went on to total 104 points from 16 matches. At the end of the campaign, Jeff took over the team captaincy upon the retirement of the great Vic Duggan, and he was to stay on board until the track closed in 1954, when he called it a day himself, having taken his overall club record to 123 league appearances, and 806 points. During his time with Harringay, he raced in three successive World Finals from 1951-53, his best performance occurring in the latter when he carded 8 points, and was the only man on the night to head eventual Champion Freddie Williams.

A great rider and a very fine gentleman was Jeff Lloyd, who served up many magical moments either side of the war for the Knowle faithful.

Competition	Matches	Points
League	38	131
National Trophy	6	15
ACU Cup	6	18
Provincial Trophy	10	46
Coronation Cup	2	10
Challenge	12	56
Bulldogs Total	**74**	**276**

William Maddern was born in 1915, and hailed from Adelaide, South Australia. He made the long journey over from his homeland to link with Bristol in 1937, a year which had seen Ronnie Greene and Fred Mockford join forces in the promotion of the West Country outfit.

The Aussie subsequently made his debut against West Ham Reserves in a challenge match at Knowle on 9 April, netting 3+2 points in a 60-23 victory. His first Provincial League appearance for the club occurred just four days later at Southampton, when he registered 2 points in a 46-38 defeat.

After that Bill quickly got to grips with the pace of British racing, and April 30 was to be a real red-letter day for him. That was when the Bulldogs entertained Leicester in a league encounter, and took their opponents to the cleaners, winning 68-15, with the tough little Australian plundering a terrific 12-point maximum. Despite the fact that this was later removed from the records upon the Midland side's resignation from the league, nothing could alter Bill's sense of joy on the night at seeing an unbeaten total against his name in the match programme. Although he never quite recaptured that form, he was a consistent scorer, and along with Fred Leavis and Rol Stobart, he supplied excellent backing to the Bulldogs heat-leader trio of Bill Rogers, Harry Shepherd and Roy Dook, as the side swept to the league title.

At Knowle, he enjoyed a particularly purple patch as the year drew to its close, scoring 12+2 points against Norwich in the Provincial Trophy, and league tallies of 9 versus both Birmingham and Norwich (again), whilst on the road, he accrued a fine 8 points in a league fixture at Liverpool on 9 September. His final figures in Provincial League racing were 85 points from 19 matches, and it would be fair to say he had learnt a lot from his first season of British racing. Two home challenge matches were arranged to complete the season, the first of which saw the Bristol boys face the might of Wembley on 5 October. Unsurprisingly, the likes of Lionel Van Praag, Tommy Price and Cliff Parkinson carried the visitors to a 65-43 success, but Bill rode his heart out to glean 10 points from 5 starts, lending terrific support to top home man Bill Rogers on a night when the rest of the Bulldogs found the pace a tad too hot. The star of the night, however, was undoubtedly Ginger Lees, who raced to an impeccable 18-point maximum for the rampant Lions. The campaign was brought to a close three evenings later, when Southampton, the Provincial League runners-up, supplied the opposition for a twelve-heat challenge match. Despite being behind for the first four heats, Bristol went on to record a relatively easy 45-27 victory, with Bill again revealing sparkling form to card 11 points. Just prior to these matches, he had a couple of outings at National League level for Wimbledon, scoring 3 points at home to Harringay on 27 September, followed by a 2+1 return at Plough Lane against New Cross on 4 October.

So, along came 1938, when the Bulldogs were promoted to the re-titled National League Division One, and having decided to stay put, Bill, like several of his team-mates, found it very hard work indeed. To all intents and purposes, it was like starting all over again in British racing, but he stuck at it manfully, and was usually good night for a few points at Knowle, his top scores being 6 against both Harringay on 22 April, and Belle Vue on 6 May. As could be expected, points were extremely hard to come by away from home, although he did enjoy one exceptionally good night against New Cross on 7 September, when he posted a tally of 7. Overall, it was a disastrous year for Bristol Speedway, with the club filling the bottom slot in the final league table, having garnered just 13 points from their 24-match programme. Bill's total for the season was 46 points from 19 matches, and with the Bulldogs subsequently dropping down to Division Two, he would surely have relished a return to a slightly lower level of racing. It wasn't to be, however, and although some sources reported him to be part of the New Cross set-up in 1939, there is no record of him having turned a wheel for the 'Frying Pan' outfit.

With the outbreak of war, little was heard of him until the 1948 season, when he indicated his willingness to give speedway another go in the UK. Perhaps, one of the reasons he hadn't appeared during the initial post-war 'boom' could be attributed to a knee injury that simply refused to heal, although he suffered from much cartilage trouble as well. It has to be said that Bristol were not amused when he was allocated to newly-formed Division Two side Edinburgh, and a dispute ensued with the Scottish club. It was to no avail though, as Bill donned the Edinburgh race-jacket for the season, and did well too, finishing up with 166 league points to his name. That was sufficient for him to occupy third position in the team's scoring, behind Dick Campbell and Eddie Lack, although their combined efforts couldn't prevent the Monarchs from finishing at the foot of the table.

Bill then went back to his native Australia, and there he stayed until 1950, when Yarmouth tempted him back for another stint in Division Two. Sadly, it wasn't a successful time for him on the East Coast and he only recorded 77 league points, and that, as the saying goes, was that for his career in British racing.

There were several amusing stories concerning Bill arriving late for meetings during his time with the Bloaters, even home ones. Just why this happened, nobody knew, but with the starting times approaching, and the Yarmouth bosses tearing out their hair, he would arrive changed and ready to race, wondering what all the fuss had been about!

Competition	Matches	Points
League	24	224
National Trophy	2	28
ACU Cup	6	$77\frac{1}{2}$
Challenge	7	75
Bulldogs Total	**39**	**$404\frac{1}{2}$**

Born to Scottish parentage in Buffalo, New York, USA, Cordy Milne first came to this country to ride in 1936. The reputation of both him and his brother Jack had most certainly gone before them, since Cordy had been crowned American Champion in both 1934 and 1935, whereas Jack had won the Australian Championship early in 1936.

Both brothers actually arrived to sign for New Cross, but once the speedway authorities had seen them in action, they posted Cordy to Hackney Wick in order to balance team strengths, thus making him one of the early 'victims' of rider control. It didn't take British supporters long to realize that he was a most able rider, since he took in his stride all tracks that were new to him, piling up impressive tallies everywhere he raced. Hackney Wick were members of the National League at the time, and this comprised of seven clubs, six of whom operated in London, with Belle Vue as the odd one out. Cordy went on to net 140 league points for the Wolves (as Hackney were nicknamed in those days) finishing third in his side's scoring. More importantly though, having scored 43 points in the so-called championship round, he qualified for the historic first staging of the World Final at Wembley Stadium on 10 September.

Joining him on speedway's night of nights were the two Hackney Wick colleagues who had finished above him in the team's league scoring, namely Dicky Case and Morian Hansen, plus brother Jack, who had fast been making a name for himself with New Cross, in spite of the unfortunate loss of a thumb in a track crash at West Ham. Cordy performed exceptionally well on the big stage, winning a couple of heats on his way to 11 points, which, when added to the 9 bonus points he carried into the meeting was sufficient for him to occupy fourth position overall, in a meeting so famously won by Australian Lionel Van Praag.

The following season, Cordy was back with Hackney Wick and he enjoyed a wonderful campaign, gleaning 222 points from a full quota of 24 league matches for an average of 9.38, as he headed the Wolves scoring. With a combined total of 71 points from the preliminary and championship rounds, he was a comfortable qualifier for the World Final on 2 September, which turned out to be a wonderful night for the American contingent, who filled the top three positions on the rostrum. Jack Milne emerged as the winner, with Wilbur Lamoreaux of Wimbledon second, while Cordy filled third spot with a dozen points, plus the 11 bonus he took into the big event. The Hackney Wick representative had to give his best to both his compatriots when they met in track combat on the night, and the only other rider to head him was 'wee' George Newton in the second heat. Not only was it a grand occasion for America, but also a great evening for London too, since the top three all rode for clubs based in the capital city.

Despite Cordy's best efforts, crowds at Hackney Wick were never that good for top-flight action, so in 1938 they opted for the cheaper running costs of the newly created Division Two. As a result, Cordy, along with team-mates Morian Hansen and the young Australian Vic Duggan, moved to Bristol, who, having won the Provincial League title, were granted promotion to the higher sphere of National League racing. The West Country outfit obviously needed to strengthen up, and the incoming three riders looked to be great acquisitions indeed. Later on, they were joined by another former Hackney Wick friend in Bill Clibbett, who had changed his mind about retiring. Upon his arrival at Knowle, Cordy was elected captain of the Bulldogs side, or perhaps it would be more accurate to say that he was nominated for the position. This was due to a really sporting gesture by the old Bristol skipper Harry Shepherd, who, upon Cordy's allocation to the club, went to see the promoters and made it clear that the American ought really to be handed the job.

It was on Good Friday 15 April, that the Bulldogs entertained New Cross in a grand 18-heat challenge match, and 17,499 speedway fans from all over the West Country flocked to Knowle Stadium for a first look at the new Bristol side. Cordy didn't disappoint them either, posting the fastest time of the evening on his way to a 12-point tally, and his sensational white-line style of riding, as well as his 'bronco' starting technique provided plenty of talking points.

The man renowned for riding the heaviest machine in the sport was to settle into a rich vein of scoring for the Bulldogs after that, although one of his finest showings occurred when Knowle Stadium played host to a World

Championship round on 24 June. The American displayed just what a fine tactician he was on a speedway bike, taking all the accolades with a 15-point maximum, his performance including the only defeat of the night over 1936 World Champion Lionel Van Praag in heat six, and an absolutely breathtaking last lap outside pass to beat George Wilks in the tenth race. In fact, it was so good that many old-time Bristol supporters used to claim it was the finest overtaking manoeuvre ever seen at Knowle.

Cordy led Bristol by example and, particularly away from home, he often carried the side. However, his efforts were unable to prevent them from ending the season in the basement position, having achieved just 6 wins and a draw. Remaining ever-present throughout the 24-match league programme, his total of 224 points included four full maximums at the Knowle raceway against Wimbledon, Wembley, Harringay and New Cross. He also returned a paid full-house (11+1) at Harringay on 23 April, in what was not only Bristol's first away league match of the season, but also turned out to be their solitary success on the road by 42 points to 41.

As if Cordy's figures weren't impressive enough, overall he represented the Bulldogs in 39 team matches during the year, yielding a tremendous total of 404½ points. On 1 September, the World Final was again staged at Wembley, with Cordy as the sole representative from Bristol. Unfortunately, on a night when Bluey Wilkinson reigned supreme, it wasn't the most fruitful meeting for the top Bulldog, as he was only able to muster a brace of wins on his way to 8 points.

In late November 1938, Bristol had a real scare, as did speedway in general, when a story circulated claiming that Cordy had been killed whilst riding in America. Happily, the rumour was false, and he, like fellow countryman Mark Twain was able to report that 'News of my death has been greatly exaggerated'.

Having endured such a difficult time, the Bulldogs subsequently opted for Division Two racing in 1939, exchanging their licence with Southampton, who were keen to sample a slice of top-tier action. Cordy duly linked with

the Saints, and significantly the move coincided with him switching to a lighter bike. This led to him being even more successful as he topped the entire league's averages on a huge figure of 11.29, having accumulated 191 points from 17 matches prior to the outbreak of war. Again, he reached the World Final, and having headed the list of qualifiers on 53 points, he was credited with eight bonus points to take into the showdown. He was a red-hot favourite to take the crown, but the outbreak of war saw the event cancelled, and probably robbed him of the sport's greatest prize.

Sadly, Cordy never returned to ride on these shores, but he later completed a hat-trick of American titles, when he again won the Championship in 1947.

Competition	Matches	Points
League	11	70
Provincial Trophy	5	33
Challenge	7	39
Bulldogs Total	**23**	**142**

Walter Morton was born on 17 January 1911, in Birmingham, West Midlands, and went on to enjoy a particularly long career in speedway.

During his time in the game, he became known as 'Wandering Wal of the Raceways', due to the fact that he didn't seem to mind who he rode for, and long-distance travelling appeared not to worry him in the slightest. An excellent example of this occurred in 1946, when both Wal and and his pre-war team-mate Bert Spencer were at Norwich. Both riders actually lived in the Norfolk town and Bert was allocated to ride for Glasgow. However, he wasn't keen on undertaking the regular journey up to Scotland, so Wal went instead, seemingly unconcerned about the weekly travel.

His time in the saddle originally began with Coventry in 1932, and he was to remain with the Warwickshire outfit the following year, when he also appeared for West Ham. He then spent the entire 1934 season with the Londoners, and although he was still with West Ham at the start of 1935, he was to finish the campaign with Wimbledon. In 1936, he linked with Bristol in the Provincial League, while continuing to 'double-up' with Wimbledon in the National League.

He made his debut for the West Country side in their first match of the season, a league encounter at Nottingham on 28 April, and whilst the Bristol camp were delighted to come away with a narrow 34-33 victory under their belts, it wasn't a memorable occasion for Wal, as he failed to open his scoring account. He then had to wait until Nottingham made the return journey on 29 May, before he made his first home appearance, but in an excellent showing he raced to a 9 point tally, playing a full part in a 43-29 success. Nottingham again provided the opposition when Bristol journeyed to the East Midlands venue for a Provincial Trophy match on 23 June, and by storming to a brilliant 12-point maximum, Wal proved that his previous performance at the track had simply been an 'off-night'.

On 7 August, a little bit of history was made when the Bristol team rode as the Bulldogs for the very first time. The programme for that evening's meeting at Knowle featured a letter from Supporters' Club member no.1289, which suggested that the team be nicknamed as such, due to the fact that other sides like Southampton and Plymouth already had monikers of their own. The Bulldogs born, they celebrated by defeating Nottingham (again) 43-29 in a league fixture, with Wal showing more good form in netting 10+1 points. Three days later, he produced a performance that really stuck out when Bristol visited Liverpool on league business. The Bulldogs lost the match 39-33, but there was no doubting that the Birmingham-born speedster was the star of the show, as he reeled off four classic wins for a super maximum. At the end of the season, Bristol, despite losing out on the League Championship to Southampton on race points difference, could be well satisfied with second spot in what, after all, was their first season of racing, with Wal's contribution to an excellent team effort being 70 points from 11 meetings.

In 1937, he began the year with Wimbledon, but it was a struggle for points in the higher sphere of British racing, and he later enjoyed a better time of things during a late-season spell with Norwich in the Provincial League.

Remaining with the Stars until the outbreak of war, Wal did a great job, particularly in 1938, when he netted 121 points from 15 league matches, with the 1939 campaign yielding 66 points from 9 meetings. As previously touched upon, he joined Glasgow in 1946, when he was appointed as captain of the side, which later acquired it's famous Tigers nickname on 22 April that year. He did well too, knocking up 131 points in Northern League racing to finish third in the Scottish outfit's scoring, behind the duo known as the 'Terrible Twins', namely Will Lowther and Joe Crowther.

Sadly, at the start of 1947, before he had even turned a wheel for Glasgow, Wal broke a leg while riding at Norwich. He was subsequently transferred to Harringay for a fee of £250. Also included in the deal were Australians Norman Lindsay and Bernard 'Bat' Byrnes, both of whom headed North to join the Tigers. Having failed to score on his league debut for Harringay in an away match at New Cross on 11 June, Wal was to go on and register 57 points from 13 matches amid the cut and thrust of Division One racing.

Although he stayed on board with the Racers the following year, opportunities were few, and he was to spend a late spell back with Norwich on loan. With hardly any appearances to speak of, it was a season to

dispel from the memory banks, and better was hoped for in 1949. Unfortunately, it didn't work out that way as he only raced in a couple of league matches for Harringay, prior to sporting the colours of Wimbledon for 8 matches during July and August, before serious injury ended his year abruptly.

Wal was to miss a complete season while he regained fitness, but in 1951 he initially made a single league appearance for Wimbledon, and then linked with newly-formed Ipswich in a series of open-licence meetings. He was later reported as having signed for Cardiff, but although programmed for a match against Poole on 23 July, he never rode for the Welsh side, instead spending some time in Division Two with Newcastle, where he recorded 84 league points, and re-acquainted himself with former Bristol team-mate Roy Dook, who was then manager of the Diamonds.

The Geordies closed their doors to speedway at the end of 1951, and Wal, still on the move, went to West Ham and rode in 28 league matches for 47 points. He then spent two unproductive seasons with Odsal (1953-54), riding in a total of just 11 league matches, before he was seemingly lost to the sport. However, he returned to the track in 1957, when he had just a handful of outings for both Norwich and Ipswich.

After missng another year, Wal was back at Ipswich in 1959, assisting the Witches during a term of Southern Area League operation. His elongated career amazingly continued on in the Provincial League with Liverpool in 1960, Middlesbrough in 1961, and then Bradford in 1962, when at the age of 51, he accumulated 131 league points.

In 1963, multi-promoter Mike Parker brought Wal back to Hackney Wick as team skipper, but time had caught up with the veteran rider, and he could only register 30 points from a dozen league matches for the Hawks.

Still he rode on in 1964, but after representing both Ipswich (again) and Weymouth, he finally hung up his racing gear, thereby ending a career had which had spanned over three decades.

Competition	Matches	Points
League	201	1,269½
National Trophy	18	135
British Speedway Cup	13	88
Anniversary Cup	15	71
Spring Cup	6	63
Challenge	56	382
4 Team Tournament	2	17
Mini-Matches	4	16
Bulldogs Total	**315**	**2041½**

Fair-haired Jack Mountford, was actually born John Mountford on 18 December 1923, in Salisbury, Wiltshire. In 1946, like a number of other future Bristol riders, he went along to Knowle Stadium for some practice and instruction as regards to becoming a speedway rider, initially on 22 July. Prior to that, he had spent many hours engaging in trials riding, and this was clearly of great value to him and most certainly played a big part in Jack's 'cinder game' ambitions.

Bristol were running open-licence meetings at the time, and having suitably impressed, Jack made his debut for the side on 30 August, scoring a single point against a composite team entitled 'The Rest'. Unfortunately, torrential rain caused the meeting to be abandoned with The Rest holding an unassailable 36-24 lead, but that didn't stop

Jack from soon establishing himself as a regular in the side. He was a 'natural', and quickly made his mark with the then Bristol boss Reg Witcomb, both with his style and a great ability to ride the white line. By the end of the season he had appeared in half-a-dozen matches, yielding a total of 32 points, with his best performance being 11+3 points versus Birmingham on 11 October.

Bristol were subsequently granted league status in 1947, happily taking their place in Division Two, alongside Birmingham, Glasgow (White City), Middlesbrough, Newcastle, Norwich, Sheffield and Wigan. Understandably, it took the Bulldogs time to settle to the vigour of regular league competition, but one of the successes was definitely Jack Mountford. He quickly found the fastest way around the Knowle racing strip, and it came as no surprise to his many fans when he finished second only to Mike Beddoe in the team's scoring, having accumulated 170 points from the 28-match league programme.

Bristol ended the year in sixth position out of the eight participating clubs, and remained in Division Two the following season, when they developed into a particularly powerful outfit. Thoroughly at home on any track, the Bulldogs swept all before them to win 23 of their 32 league matches, taking the Championship by 5 points from nearest challengers Birmingham. Having been ever-present the previous year, Jack missed just two matches along the way, netting 196 points in the process. His partnership with the lanky Fred Tuck ensured many a Bristol 5-1, and was undoubtedly one of the major factors in the side's glory charge.

Having been refused automatic promotion, Bristol begrudgingly entered another season of Division Two racing in 1949, but despite their obvious disappointment at not being amongst the elite teams, they simply carried on in the same winning vein as before. In what was a mammoth campaign, the Bulldogs partook in 44 league matches, losing just 9 times and drawing once – at Ashfield (Glasgow). Around their own circuit, Bristol were simply invincible, with Jack plundering five full maximums, as well as many other double-figure returns. He was also a member of the Bulldogs side which famously recorded the maximum score possible, when they defeated Glasgow (White City) 70-14 on 7 October. Jack recorded 9 points in that total, but was paid for 12, being unbeaten by an opponent after following his partner home in three rides. Ever-present throughout the elongated league campaign, the end of season statistics showed he had enjoyed his best year since joining the club, with 382½ points to his name. That total was sufficient for him to again finish second in the team's scoring, behind skipper Billy Hole, who notched a massive 429 points.

In 1950, Bristol were at last granted promotion to Division One, and at the end of the term, Jack could rightly be deemed as one of few successes in what was a difficult campaign. The Bulldogs management made several bids to augment their riding strength, but apart from the acquisition of Geoff Pymar, their hard work unfortunately went up blind alleys, and the side ended up in seventh position out of nine teams. Jack was riding some of the away tracks for the very first time, and it was no surprise that his scoring was reduced against some of the sport's top riders.

Even so, he still did very well to finish up with 169 points, once again remaining ever-present throughout 32 league matches. As had happened in the past, knowledge of their home circuit, plus a marvellous team spirit, paved the way for many successes at Knowle, with 14 victories out of 16 matches. It was a different story to report from their travels, however, with a solitary 47-37 win at Harringay on 8 September. If only Bristol could have signed another rider or two, used to racing at the very top level, Jack would surely have done much better, but he was under pressure all the time due to the struggles that some of his team-mates endured.

Remaining in the top-flight, 1951 was to be much the same as the previous year, although the Bulldogs did climb a rung to finish in sixth position. Jack missed just one league match over the course of the season, but increased his scoring to 186 points, which represened a very good effort indeed.

The 1952 season was again a case of 'the mixture as before', with Bristol occupying eighth position in Division One. Jack was as consistent as ever though, appearing in every league match for the fourth time in six

seasons, while netting another 166 points, the high spot being a tally of 10+1 at home to Odsal on 9 May.

During the winter months Jack gave much thought to his future – he'd been at Bristol since 1946, and wondered if a change of track would benefit him. 'Perhaps I've been here too long', he was reported as saying, and the Bristol

promoters, mindful of his splendid service to the club, allowed him to leave for Division Two side Leicester in time for the 1953 season.

Sadly, things just didn't work out and it wasn't long before he was struggling badly. His total league points amounted to just 66 for his new team, and in his absence, the Bulldogs slumped to the basement position in Division One, leaving many Bristol supporters to rue his departure.

In 1954, Jack garnered only 5 points for Leicester, prior to moving on to South-ampton, but try as he might, he couldn't find form with the Saints, and called it day after scoring just a dozen league points for the Hampshire outfit.

There is no doubt whatsoever that Jack was one of the finest riders who ever donned a Bristol race-jacket, for he gave the club seven great years of loyal service, and often turned out when he should have been resting an injury. He was also a fast rider, and this was perhaps best emphasized in 1948, when the Bristol riders took part in an individual meeting for the Silver Trophy at Poole on 31 May. In the opening heat, Jack set a new track record of 80.4 seconds for the 420-yard circuit, when beating his regular team-mates Billy Hole, Eric Salmon and Roger Wise. It proved to be a grand night all round for Bristol, since Jack eventually finished as runner-up to fellow Bristol teamster Fred Tuck, while Roger Wise grabbed third position on the podium. This was one of many achievements earned by Jack Mountford, a true Bulldog in every sense of the word.

Competition	Matches	Points
League	8	78
National Trophy	3	50
Challenge	3	25
Bulldogs Total	**14**	**153**

Having been born in Stockholm, Sweden on 11 November 1929, Harald-Olof Ingemar Nygren was to enjoy a long and distinguished career in speedway, throughout which he was always known as Olle. The blonde-haired son of a chemist began his speedway career in 1947, after trying both road racing and car racing.

It was in 1951, that he burst upon the scene in Britain, making his National League Division One debut for Harringay on 22 June, in a home match ironically against Bristol. Olle was to appear in only 10 league matches for the Racers, netting 76 points, and one can only wonder what sort of figures he would have returned, had he been with them for the entire season? After such an outstanding entry, Olle could have walked into any Division One side to fill a heat-leader role, but there were strict rules in those days and it wasn't allowed, at least not on a permanent basis.

After missing a year of British racing, he returned to these shores with New Cross in 1953. Sadly, in June that year, promoter Fred Mockford was forced to close the doors of the Old Kent Road venue to the sport since crowds had fallen, and he was losing money. The New Cross supremo had wanted to make Olle a permanent signing, but had been turned down by officialdom, with the brilliant Swede only permitted to race on a short-term basis. At the time of the track's premature closure, he had ridden in 11 Coronation Cup matches for the Rangers, gleaning a total of 102 points.

It is worth mentioning at this juncture, that Bristol, who were toiling amongst the elite of Division One racing, could have been strengthened considerably by signing some of the former New Cross boys, but strangely that didn't happen.

However, the Bulldogs did fight long and hard to be allowed to sign Olle, and in July, promoter George Allen was able to state that he had reached an agreement to acquire his services, albeit for a short while due to restrictions laid down by the Ministry of Labour. Even then, there was a lot of 'red tape', as the Control Board wanted to consider the counter claims that other teams had for the Swede, despite the fact that the Bristol promoter already had his signature on a contract! So instead of being able to represent Bristol in the National Trophy at Odsal, Olle travelled to Belle Vue for the £500 Gold Cup individual event, and duly defeated Jack Parker in a run-off for the title.

After again putting his case forward, George Allen finally received clearance for Olle to make his debut as a Bulldog on 17 July, in a home league match against West Ham. The inclusion of a world-class racer clearly gave the Bristol team a tremendous boost, as they blasted to a 62-22 win on a rain-soaked circuit. Olle could not have enjoyed a more sparkling debut, revealing great track craft as he plundered a paid maximum (11+1 points). A week later, Norwich provided the opposition on National Trophy business, and the crowd of 7,590 witnessed the real power of the Swedish flyer as he ripped to an 18-point maximum in a 64-44 victory. The following evening, he netted a paid 16 point tally (15+1) in the second leg, and helped ensure Bristol's safe passage through to the semi-final, where they faced Wimbledon.

Sadly, Olle wasn't able to return from his homeland for the first leg against the Dons at Knowle on 7 August, with the Bulldogs subsequently suffering a 62-46 reverse. Had he ridden, the result could have been so very different, for at the Plough Lane home of Wimbledon, the speedy Sweede ended the return leg with a magnificent paid full-house (17+1) to his name. Unfortunately, his efforts couldn't prevent Bristol from tumbling out, but his personal record in the competition was worthy of note, with 50+2 points accumulated in just 3 meetings!

Olle was only able to ride in a few league matches, which was a disappointment for the Bulldogs and their supporters, but when he was available, he added some real fire-power. In fact, he rode in just 8 Division One fixtures as things turned out, his total of 78 points including a full-house talley against Belle Vue at Knowle on 31 July, plus of course the previously mentioned paid maximum against West Ham on his debut.

During his brief stint with Bristol, there was one other event of note that created much interest for the West Country fans, namely his appearance in the World Final at Wembley on 17 September. Producing wonderful form in what was actually his debut in the sport's most prestigious meeting, he raced to a dozen points, necessitating a run-off for third place with Wimbledon's Geoff Mardon.

Unfortunately, for the Bristol contingent, the extra race resulted in a win for the Swede's opponent, with a battling Olle falling and remounting on the final lap, thereby having to settle for fourth place overall.

The Bulldogs applied for, and were granted Division Two racing in 1954, so any chance of Olle Nygren returning were reduced to nil – it simply wouldn't have been allowed in those days. He did, however, continue to ply his trade in British racing, serving several other teams with distinction, namely: Wimbledon (1954); Southampton (1960); Swindon (1962); Norwich (1962-64); Wimbledon (1965-68); West Ham (1969-71); Ipswich (1972-74); Coventry (1974) and King's Lynn (1975). In the World Final, he made a further four appearances on the 'big night' (1954, 1955, 1958 and 1959), with his best showing occurring in 1954, when he recorded 13 points, and finished in third spot after Wembley's Brian Crutcher had beaten him in a run-off for the runner-up position.

Competition	Matches	Points
League	27	134
National Trophy	4	22
Southern Shield	6	23
Challenge	8	19
Bulldogs Total	**45**	**198**

Thomas Oakley was born in Southampton, Hampshire in 1910, and was the elder brother of Bob, who began riding at New Cross after the war, prior to enjoying a distinguished shale career with Southampton (1947-50), Wembley (1950-52), Norwich (1954) and Wolverhampton (1961).

It is somewhat unusual for an older brother to begin racing after his younger sibling, but that is exactly what happened with Tom in 1948, when he took his first skids around his hometown track at the age of 37. However, he wasn't a complete novice as far as motorcycle competition was concerned, since, like his brother, he had been a regular grass-tracker – it was simply that Tom decided on a speedway career later than most.

Despite this, he worked hard at his game, and was without doubt one of the finest discoveries of the year as he piled up an impressive total of 209 points in league matches for the Saints. Being built like a boxer, Tom was a tough opponent, and whilst he was always scrupulously fair in his riding, he proved extremely difficult to shift from the racing line.

In 1949, he again sported the body colour of Southampton, and continued to make up for lost time by racking up another 228 league points. Remembering that the Saints had been promoted from Division Three to Division Two, it made Tom's progress all the more remarkable, given the fact he wasn't far off his fortieth birthday!

In a move that upset the Southampton faithful, his brother joined Wembley for £1,500 mid-way through the 1950 campaign, and it was almost as though Tom thought he'd have to do his bit to cover the loss. Spurred on, he plundered 212 points from a shortened league programme, finishing just 5 points behind top man Jimmy Squibb in the side's scoring. One of his proudest moments undoubtedly occurred in the Hants and Dorset Cup at Poole on 22 May, when he established a new track record of 74.8 seconds as the Saints raced to a 52-32 success.

Unfortunately, Southampton were forced to close down in July 1951, due to the crippling effects of the ludicrous enter-tainment tax that speedway was saddled with. Having netted 59 points, Tom occupied pole position in the Saints league scoring at the time, and he subsequently decided to try his luck in the top division, joining New Cross. He did well for the Rangers too, gleaning 81 points from 15 matches for a healthy 6.27 average, thus proving he could do the business at the highest level. With Bristol struggling, it was surprising that he linked with New Cross as the West

Country outfit could most definitely have done with his services, though it's fair to say that the Bulldogs received very little help from officialdom.

However, although Tom began the 1952 campaign as a New Cross rider, after appearing in 17 league matches for 63 points, he did finally did join Bristol for a fee of £600, after expressing a desire to find a club nearer his Southampton home.

Somewhat ironically, he made his debut for the Bulldogs in a league match against New Cross at Knowle on 20 June, scoring 7 points in a 47-37 victory. He was to settle into a useful scoring vein for his new club, and although the high spot was a paid maximum (11+1 points) in a home match against Norwich on 1 August, he was generally more consistent on the away circuits. It was a coincidence, but Tom went on to also accumulate 63 points for Bristol, as he had done earlier in the season for New Cross, although the tally was accrued from 4 fewer league meetings for the West Country side.

In 1953, things didn't start too well for him, and in referring back to a crash at West Ham on 26 August the previous year, he was quoted as saying 'I hope I shall not get anymore headaches'. Sadly, he crashed in a pre-season practice at Knowle, suffering a chipped bone in his foot, which was to put him out of action until May. Once fit, he was restricted to mainly second-half outings, and only actually represented the Bulldogs in a couple of home league matches, scoring 3 points against Wimbledon on 10 July, and 4+1 when West Ham supplied the opposition one week later. Unfortunately, Bristol finished bottom of the league, and the year didn't hold many happy memories for either the rider or the club.

Tom wasn't finished with the sport though, and with the Bulldogs dropping into Division Two for 1954, he was determined to show the Knowle regulars what he could do. Whilst he never quite revealed his old Southampton form, he did secure 64 points from 12 league matches, with a tally of 9+2 being his best effort when the Saints visited Knowle Stadium on 13 August. He certainly tried hard, but somehow lacked consistency, though the fact that he was in his mid-40s should also be taken into consideration.

Tom called it a day at the end of the campaign in order to concentrate on his business interests in Southampton, but it has to be said that for a man who began the sport late, he certainly made up for lost time. Like many of the riders who proudly wore the orange and black colours of Bristol, he always gave of his best for the club.

Competition	Matches	Points
League	132	742
National Trophy	18	105
Coronation Cup	13	56
Southern Shield	9	39
Challenge	45	253
4 Team Tournament	2	22
Mini-Matches	2	5
Bulldogs Total	**221**	**1,222**

Geoffrey Pymar was born in Eye, Suffolk on 14 February 1912, and his interest in racing began in 1931, when he attended grass-track events at Diss, and was also a spectator at the opening grass-cum-speedway meeting at the site that was to become the Firs Stadium, Norwich on 18 August.

A couple of years were to pass before Geoff decided to do something about becoming a rider himself, eventually contacting both Crystal Palace and Norwich for trials. Whilst he was having rides at the latter circuit, he received an approach from West Ham, and it was reported at the time that he was hoping to get fixed up with the London outfit as he found the prospect of racing on the big, sweeping Custom House track very appealing indeed. However, believing that 'a bird in the hand is worth two in the bush', Geoff was quick to accept an offer from Wimbledon, and was to remain with the club right up to the outbreak of war in 1939.

During his time with the Dons, he found himself paired with the legendary Vic Huxley (a Wimbledon rider from 1931-36), and there can be no doubt that the young Geoff Pymar learned much from the brilliant Australian.

After making his England debut against Australia at Wimbledon on 9 July 1934, Geoff was to again represent his country against the Aussies the following year, whilst in between also taking part in the Test series down under. He later went on to race for England versus USA at Wimbledon on 30 August 1937, prior to appearing in home series against Australia in 1938 and 1939, plus another away tour in 1938/39. On the individual front, Geoff once made it through to the Star Championship final in 1935, scoring 3 points, while the one time he qualified for a World Final occurred in 1938, when he managed just a brace of points.

After the hostilities, he linked with New Cross in 1946, and enjoyed an excellent season with the Rangers, plundering 164 points from 19 National League matches.

Geoff continued to ply his trade with New Cross the following year, and although he experienced a loss of form for a time, he battled on gamely and remained ever-present throughout the 24-match league programme to net a total of 163 points. At the time, the World Championship was 'on hold' until 1949, but the British Riders' Championship was held in its place, and in 1947 Geoff qualified for the Wembley showdown on 11 September, netting a 4-point tally. He really showed what he could do at West Ham on 7 October, however, when against a class field, he triumphed in the Cundy Trophy. The quiet man from Suffolk, who had a semi leg-trailing style was again based at the 'Frying Pan' (the quaint nickname for the tiny New Cross track) in 1948, when he showed flashes of his best form on his way to a tally of $116\frac{1}{2}$ points from 21 league fixtures.

A reported fee of £1,250 changed hands in 1949, when Geoff moved across London to join Harringay, and he certainly injected a bit of 'bite' to the Racers side as he piled up 232 league points. Whilst riding for Harringay, he reminded his former team-mates and supporters at New Cross that he was still a force to be reckoned with, blasting to a 12-point maximum when the Rangers visited on 9 September, having previously registered a brilliant 11 points in the corresponding away fixture on 3 August.

It was in 1950, that Bristol gained promotion to Division One of speedway's National League, and the Bulldogs management made sterling efforts to strengthen their side for the tougher level of competition. However, it seemed that every rider they approached just wasn't interested in moving to the West Country to ride – all except Geoff Pymar that is. After beginning the season with Harringay, and scoring 19 points from 4 league meetings, he was purchased by Bristol boss George Allen, with a cheque for £1,000 changing hands. His signing certainly helped to bolster the Bulldogs, and they needed it badly, since Fred Tuck retired almost as soon as he arrived.

Geoff's club debut took place in a home league encounter against New Cross on 9 June, when he notched a paid 5 point tally (4+1) in front of 14,180 fans, but was unable to save Bristol from suffering a narrow 43-41 reverse. The timing of the defeat was quite unbelievable really, for it was the first time the Bulldogs had been beaten in a league match at Knowle since Middlesbrough had won on 29 August 1947.

Following that, Geoff was to prove a steady scorer for the side, accumulating a total of

$115\frac{1}{2}$ points from 23 league matches, with the highlight being a paid 11 point (9+2) return against former club Harringay, when they visited Knowle on 9 September. The previous evening had also been one to savour, for despite only scoring 4 points on his return to Harringay, his contribution helped Bristol to a 47-37 victory, this being their solitary away success of a very difficult year in top-flight racing. Geoff was to have one of his best-ever years in the sport in 1951, as he became very much the master of the 290-yard Knowle circuit – only three times failing to record double-figures. Ever-present throughout the 32 league fixtures, his season's total of 271 points saw him finish just ahead of Dick Bradley at the head of the Bulldogs points chart.

His tall scoring tailed-off somewhat in 1952, although he still registered 209 points from 35 matches to occupy third place in the club's figures behind Dick Bradley and Chris Boss.

Sadly, Bristol endured a nightmare in 1953, slipping down to the basement position in the Division One table. Geoff often struggled, mustering just 44 league points from 15 matches. Internationally, he was again recognized by England, being named as reserve for a Test match against New Zealand at Bristol on 25 September, although in the event he didn't get a ride. On the team front, things improved the following season, when, having dropped back into Division Two, the Bulldogs claimed the Championship, finish-ing 4 points ahead of nearest challengers Poole. The year proved to be a little better for Geoff too, as he appeared in all 20 league matches, however, a tally of $75\frac{1}{2}$ points wasn't good by his standards. Bristol raced to poor crowds in 1955, eventually closing pre-maturely in June, and the general malaise was reflected in Geoff's racing as his best form eluded him, with just 27 points garnered from 7 matches.

Following the Bulldogs demise, many folk thought that Geoff would retire from racing, but they couldn't have been more wrong! In 1956, he joined Norwich and was to spend two seasons on board with the Stars, during which time he knocked up 93 league points in their colours. Again, he was thought to have retired when he didn't appear in 1958, and this seemed to be confirmed by another non-riding year in 1959. However, upon the formation of the Provincial League in 1960, Geoff re-emerged as a member of the Yarmouth team, and he did well for the Bloaters, netting 131½ points as he formed a formidable spearhead alongside Ivor Brown and Johnny Fitzpatrick.

Unfortunately, the Norfolk operation closed to league racing after one year, instead running open-licence meetings, so Geoff moved on to Middlesbrough. Due to the excessive travelling, his stint in the North East was short-lived, and after a spell out of the saddle, he was later identified with Wolverhampton for a time.

One final change saw him race for Bradford at the Greenfield Autodrome in 1962, but when they closed at the end of the season, he really did hang up his leathers for good, having tallied 107 league points. That brought the curtain down on a career that had incredibly spanned three decades, and having retired from active service to one sport, he was then identified with another as he became a golf caddy and was spotted on courses the world over, accompanying 1969 Open Championship victor Tony Jacklin.

Much later on, Geoff was honoured by the Veteran Speedway Riders' Association, being elected their President for 2002, but sadly he was ill in hospital with a terminal illness. Nevertheless, some of his old friends appeared at his bedside, and the chain of office was put around his neck. He passed away soon

afterwards, but as a mark of respect at the VSRA Dinner, the chain of office was placed on the empty President's chair. It was a moving tribute of which everyone felt Geoff would have approved.

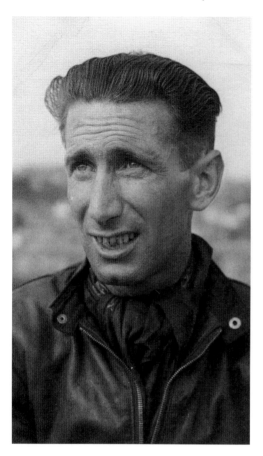

Competition	Matches	Points
League	50	169
National Trophy	4	15
British Speedway Cup	14	74
Anniversary Cup	13	62
Challenge	12	44
Bulldogs Total	**93**	**364**

Born Cecil James Quick in Taunton, Somerset on 19 January 1919, this West Country lad was known throughout his speedway career as Cyril. His racing career began on the grass-track circuits in 1937, and he was to meet with some degree of success, until joining the forces at the outbreak of the war.

Cyril enjoyed his first taste of speedway at one of the Monday night practice sessions at Knowle Stadium in 1946, and continued to train as a pupil at Tiger Stevenson's school. Cyril proved a fast learner, so much so in fact that he was handed a team spot for the Bulldogs opening match of the 1947 season, an away Division Two encounter at Middlesbrough on 10 April, when he record-ed 2+1 points in a 61-23 reverse. His home debut occurred the following evening and he managed to glean another couple of points as Bristol again tasted defeat by 57 points to 49 against Birmingham in a challenge match.

Despite his inexperience, Cyril was to show plenty of spirit and justifiably held down a regular team spot throughout the campaign. After six successive losses, the Bulldogs finally claimed their first victory of the season on 2 May, when Middlesbrough were beaten 47-35 in a league fixture at Knowle, and Cyril's contribution was a well-taken 6+1 points. As the weeks passed by, his knowledge increased and he picked up many useful points; one of the high spots being his home showing against Sheffield in the Division Two section of the British Speedway Cup on 23 May. Bristol lost the match 50-44, but with five starts yielding 12 points, Cyril gave an outstanding performance, and it seemed it would be only a matter of time before he became a top-line rider. To complete a wonderful personal evening, the mechanic by trade, further enhanced his growing reputation when roaring to victory over the Sheffield duo of Tommy Bateman and Bruce Semmens in the second-half Senior Scratch Race final.

At the close of the season, Cyril had every reason to be pleased with his own efforts, for he had remained ever-present during the 28-match league campaign, netting exactly 100 points in the process. Much was expected as he again lined-up for the Bulldogs in 1948, but as so often happens to riders, it was to be a case of simply 'standing still'. Cyril gleaned a total of just 69 points from 22 league matches, his two best performances being scores of 9+2 and 9+1 in home meetings against Sheffield (14 May) and Fleetwood (4 June) respectively.

Although he always put in plenty of endeavour, much of the previous season's sparkle was missing, and it came as little surprise, when, at the end of August, he requested a transfer away from Bristol for 'personal reasons'. At the time, the rider explained that he had no problem with his team-mates or the management, but felt a Division Three track might be beneficial to his progress. Negotiations then took place for Cyril to join Yarmouth, but the Control Board refused to allow the move since the transfer deadline had passed.

However, the next thing the loyal Bulldogs supporters knew was that Cyril was lining up for Poole in a Division Three encounter at Hull on 11 September, when he netted 7 points. The Control Board had apparently given 'special dispensation' for his move, as the Dorset outfit had suffered a number of injuries to key riders, so needed strengthening as a matter of urgency. Cyril subsequently made his home debut for the Pirates against Coventry two evenings later, when he raced to a brilliant 11 points in a 47-37 defeat, only missing out on a maximum when losing to visiting skipper Bob Fletcher in his final ride.

On 14 September, the Pirates visited Yarmouth for a league match, and one cannot help but wonder what the fans of the Norfolk side must have thought when they noted that riding for Poole was Cyril Quick, whom they had every reason to believe would actually be representing their beloved Bloaters! They also saw very quickly what they were missing, since Cyril sped to an impressive 10-point tally, although he was unable to prevent his team from losing 45-39.

Sadly, his spell in Poole's colours was to be brief in 1948, as he suffered a broken leg in a grass-track meeting, rendering him out of action for the remainder of the season.

Having returned to fitness, he was back with Poole for both 1949 and 1950, when he not only captained the side, but was a true 'tower of strength', recording league tallies of $386\frac{1}{2}$ points and 322 respectively.

In 1951, Cyril requested a transfer, and after a hefty fee had changed hands, he linked with Oxford, who had been promoted to Division Two as a result of winning the Division Three

Championship. However, for reasons that remained a mystery, he just couldn't settle with the Cheetahs. Before he had ridden a single league match for them, he was loaned out to Yarmouth (who were then a Division Two side) for whom he registered 142 league points and recovered some of his best form.

In 1952, the Poole co-promoter Len Matchan, who had unsuccessfully tried to persuade Cyril to remain a Pirate the previous year, became involved in the running of Southern League side Wolverhampton. Straight away, he began to strengthen what was a woefully weak team, and one rider he immediately thought of was Cyril Quick, who didn't hesitate in putting pen to paper. He enjoyed a great season too, accumulating $272\frac{1}{2}$ points from league matches alone, as he finished above Benny King at the head of the club's scoring.

Having regained all his old sparkle, great things were expected from Cyril in 1953, but it wasn't to be as he made the decision to retire in order to concentrate on his business interests. He could, however, be happy that he had bowed out on a high note.

Competition	Matches	Points
League	13	141
Provincial League KOC	4	70
Challenge	5	53
Bulldogs Total	**22**	**264**

Trevor John Redmond was born in Christchurch, New Zealand on 16 June 1927, and interestingly a 'Who's Who' of the sport once compiled by the *Speedway Echo*, listed his permanent job in his native land as a wool classer.

He first became interested in speedway racing at Canterbury (NZ) in 1948. It soon became obvious that Trevor was a 'natural', and his progress was so rapid that he finished as runner-up to the one and only Bruce Abernethy in the 1950 New Zealand Championship, after which, he was to make his way over to Britain.

At the time, Aldershot were team building as they had been elected to Division Three of the National League, and their manager George Saunders was only too pleased to give the mustard-keen Kiwi a trial. Trevor was promptly signed up for the newly formed side and he soon became the master of the strangely shaped 302-yard Aldershot circuit.

He not only became the leading scorer for the Hampshire side, but was also the brightest light in the entire division, amassing a total of 342 league points to finish just ahead of Oxford's Pat Clarke. However, in a reversal of that situation, Trevor then had to be content with the runner-up position behind the Oxford rider in the Division Three Riders' Championship at Walthamstow, having garnered 13 points.

In 1951, he remained on board with the Shots to pile up another 344 league points, won the Division Three Match Race Championship, shattered track records galore, and represented his country at C level against England. Small wonder that the higher sphere of racing beckoned, and in 1952, whilst Bristol needed his services dearly and were prepared to shell out a sizeable fee, it was Wembley who he signed for.

Trevor was to stay with the Lions until they closed down at the end of 1956, during which time he gave sterling service, scoring 708 points from 122 league matches. While with the famous London club, he was non-riding reserve at the 1952 World Final, prior to taking what turned out to be his only rides in the big event two years later, when he netted a 5 point tally.

In 1957, he rode for non-league Yarmouth, and when Birmingham moved their operation to Bradford Trevor also helped out the Tudors. He didn't ride at all the following year, preferring to stay on the other side of the fence having brought the sport back to St Austell.

In 1959, he reappeared on the racing scene for Swindon, but sadly he was a shadow of the rider who had once held the track record at

Blunsdon (in 1951) and he only mustered a total of 37 points from 12 league matches.

Another change then saw Trevor link with Bristol in the new Provincial League in 1960, and showing his old touch, the Kiwi announced his arrival in grand style by blasting to a 12-point maximum on his club debut against Stoke at Knowle Stadium on 20 May. He went on to race in a total of 13 league matches, racking up 141 points for a huge 10.92 average as he helped Bristol to third place in the final table, just a couple of points adrift of Rayleigh and Poole – the Essex outfit taking title by virtue of a superior race points difference. Trevor produced many breathtaking performances along the way, including further dozen-point full-houses in away matches at Bradford and Sheffield, as well as one in the home encounter against Poole. Meanwhile, in the Provincial League Knock-Out Cup, his form was remarkable, starting with an 18-point maximum at Bradford in the first round, prior to plundering 16 points in the semi-final at Edinburgh.

The Bulldogs then travelled to Rayleigh for the first leg of the final on 9 September, and although Trevor put on a wonder show to register an unbeaten 18 points, he couldn't prevent a 52-41 defeat. Bristol weren't to be denied though, and raced to a 59-37 success in the second leg on 23 September, thereby giving them the trophy by an aggregate score of 100 points to 89. It was Trevor's form that again caught the eye of those present, for he amazingly racked up another six-ride maximum, giving him a total of 70 points out of a possible 72 in a glorious cup run. There was more to celebrate the very next evening too, when Trevor scooped the Provincial League Riders' Championship at Cradley Heath, with as fine a 15-point full-house as anyone is ever likely to see.

With Knowle Stadium unfortunately closing down for good, Trevor stuck to promoting the sport at St Austell (as he had done since 1958) and Dublin (Shelbourne Park) in 1961, but did return to the saddle for a late-season stint with Wolverhampton.

Then, in 1962, came a real triumph, when he opened a new track at Neath, in West Glamorgan, and led his team to second place in the Provincial League. His achievement being brilliantly summed up by speedway journalist Cyril J. Hart: 'Trevor Redmond created something out of nothing, put a team of nobodies on a strange track, rode with them, captained them, managed them, and convinced them they were better than any other crowd.'

In 1963, he was again promoting at St Austell, although he was to also don his leathers for the Gulls, and in 1964, he filled similar roles on and off the track after re-introducing the sport at Glasgow's White City Stadium.

Trevor was to stay in place at the Scottish venue for three seasons in all, the latter two years being as promoter only, with Danny Taylor subsequently taking over the controlling reigns in time for the 1967 season.

That wasn't the end of Trevor's speedway involvement, however, as in 1970, he played an important role in the re-introduction of league racing at Wembley Stadium – a venture that would last for two seasons.

Worthy of mention is one other important task that was undertaken by Trevor, or 'Fats' as his friends dubbed him, and it happened in 1952, when he became the nominated guardian of a young New Zealand boy who came here to try his luck, namely . . . Barry Briggs.

Competition	Matches	Points
League	55	375
National Trophy	6	35
Provincial Trophy	19	203
ACU Cup	6	44
Coronation Cup	4	$34\frac{1}{2}$
Challenge	22	146
Bulldogs Total	**112**	**$837\frac{1}{2}$**

William Rogers was born in St Kilda, Australia in 1911, and began his speedway career in 1930. Just two years later, he caused something of a sensation by winning his country's national Championship.

Bill subsequently came to ride here in the United Kingdom in 1934, with a reputation of being the most talkative Australian rider ever to visit these shores. Indeed, his friends used to say he could talk for his nation against any opposition, but nevertheless he was a cheerful chap, as well as being a rider with a spectacular crowd-pleasing style.

He was, however, to attain a most unwelcome 'wild' tag, as he became one of the unluckiest men in the game, being involved in several accidents, often through no fault of his own. The first such incident occurred in his initial season of British racing, when he suffered a broken ankle whilst riding for Wimbledon.

Bill then went to the United States for a spell, but in 1936, he returned to Britain and signed for Bristol. It soon became obvious that Ronnie Greene had acquired a most able rider for his new side, and as the season unfolded, the West Country supporters were to appreciate just how good he was. The Provincial League programme began at Nottingham on 28 April, and in a great start for both rider and club, Bill netted 8 points in a narrow 34-33 success.

By and large, he continued to make good contributions thereafter, with two meetings against Plymouth particularly standing out. The first of these was an away league fixture on 7 July, when he starred with an unbeaten 11+1 tally in a 37-35 victory. Later in the year, when the Devon side made their second league visit of the campaign to Knowle Stadium on 18 September, the Bulldogs, as they had been nicknamed early the previous month, went on the rampage to win 49-23, with both Bill and his compatriot Eric Collins hitting 12-point maximums.

In all, the man from St Kilda was to appear in 15 league matches, gleaning a total of 93 points as Bristol went on to just miss out on the title, instead having to settle for the runner-up spot behind Southampton on race points difference.

Staying with the Bulldogs the following season, the Aussie was to become the club's leading rider, as he remained ever-present throughout the 20-match league programme to score 200 points and steer his side to Championship glory. In a year to savour, Bill actually recorded slightly more points on his travels than he did at Knowle, his away tally of 101 points including four-ride maximums at Liverpool and Birmingham. He also put together three full-house performances at home, with Nottingham, Norwich and Birmingham on the receiving end. Meanwhile, paid maximums were carded in home and away matches against Leicester (11+1, and 10+2 respectively), and also against Norwich (10+2) at Knowle; although the points gained against Leicester weren't included in the season's final figures due to the Midland track's early closure.

His scoring was excellent by any standards, and it was little surprise that from the end of July onwards, he 'doubled-up' with Wimbledon in the National League, registering 48 points from 10 matches.

The season also saw Bill honoured when selected for his country in a Test match against England at Knowle on 30 July. Before an audience of 12,723, he raced to 12+4 points as the Australians simply overwhelmed their hosts by a staggering 79-29 scoreline. A further Test match saw Australia face America at the Bristol raceway on 24 September, when Bill's efforts earned 8+1 points in a $64\frac{1}{2}$-$43\frac{1}{2}$ victory for his side, before an increased attendance of 14,300.

In 1938, the leagues were re-titled and the Bulldogs deservedly gained Division One status after their efforts of the previous year. Understandably, Bill was retained, and the side was strengthened by the arrival of four ex-Hackney Wick riders, namely Cordy Milne, Morian Hansen, Vic Duggan and Bill Clibbett. Unfortunately, like most of the Bristol boys who had done so well in the Provincial League, Bill found it hard to gather points. There were some notable showings though, like a 9-point return against visiting West Ham on 2 September, and an even better 11 points against New Cross a week later. Meanwhile, on the team's travels, his best performance of the year occurred at New Cross on 25 May, when a good evening's work

yielded 9+1 points. One other performance that really stood out happened at Knowle on 3 June, when Belle Vue visited for an ACU Cup match, and were sent packing as the men in orange and black went on the offensive to win 74-34, with the gritty Australian notching a 13-point tally. In the final analysis of the season, Bill had ridden in 20 league matches, recording 103 points, as the Bulldogs ended up occupying the bottom position of the seven participating sides.

It must be said that Bill rode as well as any of his team-mates who were ex-Provincial League lads, and he went home confident of a return in 1939, when Bristol unsurprisingly dropped back into Division Two. Sadly, this didn't materialize as he suffered a badly broken leg, and was thought to be lost to the sport for good.

However, after the war, Bill began riding again, and in 1948, he returned to 'Blighty' to ride for Belle Vue in Division One of the National League. Misfortune struck again though when, in a bizarre accident on the very day he landed in the UK, he fractured a toe whilst going upstairs to bed. He subsequently went on to score 28 league points from 12 matches for the Aces, but didn't pull up any trees and was transferred to Wimbledon for £60.

As if to prove that bad luck just wouldn't leave him alone, he then broke a collarbone whilst having a practice spin, and only got to appear in a single league match for the Dons at home to Wembley on 23 August, when he failed to score from 2 outings.

In 1949, after a rough time with the Londoners, which yielded a single point from 3 league matches, Bill moved on to link with Southampton in Division Two. Although he garnered 27 points, he was not the rider of old; like so many other riders, the war had taken years out of his career and that, together with his unlucky run of injuries, saw him return home and retire from active speedway. He will, however, always be remembered for his 1937 season with Bristol, when he was very much the top dog.

Competition	Matches	Points
League	204	1,159½
National Trophy	25	175
British Speedway Cup	14	87
Anniversary Cup	16	87
Spring Cup	2	8
Coronation Cup	16	76
Challenge	53	330
Mini-Matches	2	11
4 Team Tournament	1	4
Bulldogs Total	**333**	**1,937½**

Born in Bath, Somerset, on 30 January 1918, Eric Salmon went on to become a very keen and able grass-track rider, prior to having speedway trials at the Birmingham training schools in the winter of 1946/47. After making good progress, he signed for Bristol, and his arrival meant yet another local boy had been recruited to the Bulldogs line-up. Eric also made it a real family affair, when, having married their sister, he became the brother-in-law of team-mates Billy, Johnny and Graham Hole.

Prior to the start of the 1947 season, Eric had impressed with his ability to ride the white line in trials at Knowle Stadium, and was deservedly handed a team spot as a result. He duly made his club debut in Bristol's first match of the year, a Division Two league encounter at Middlesbrough on 10 April, and although he failed to trouble the scorers, he rode with plenty of fighting spirit.

Eric was good for a few points in the majority of matches as the season progressed, and despite his tough, all-action style which often saw him suffer nasty knocks, he was just one appearance short of attending every fixture throughout the Bulldogs 28-match league programme. Those of course were the days of no guest riders, no rider replacement facilities, and no special dispensations, meaning that if a team was hit by injuries they simply had to soldier on as best they could. That is exactly what Eric did, with his loyalty to the team emphasized when he badly damaged a knee, but carried on riding, having had a special brace made.

The highlight of his league campaign was a 12-point maximum against Glasgow at Knowle on 15 August, while he also weighed in with a 10+1 tally when Birmingham visited on 17 October. Looking at the end-of-term statistics, Eric finished with a total of 126 league points to his name, which represented a sound effort in his first season of racing. One other meeting that was particularly special occurred at Knowle on 18 July, when Wigan provided the opposition for a British Speedway Cup encounter. The Bristol club was honoured to have the popular comedy film star duo of Stan Laurel and Oliver Hardy in attendance, and Eric certainly impressed the illustrious pair by racing to 14 points in a 52-44 victory, his only defeat coming at the hands of Jack Gordon in heat eleven.

Still with the Bulldogs in 1948, Eric and the team were to enjoy a wonderful year as they stormed to the League Championship by a 5-point margin from their nearest challengers Birmingham. Not only did the man from Bath ride in the full quota of 32 Division Two matches for 213 points, but he also appeared in all 50 official meetings undertaken by the Bulldogs over the year, netting 313 points in total. In forming a potent spearhead alongside Fred Tuck, Billy Hole, Roger Wise and Jack Mountford, Eric scorched to 4 full maximums around his home strip in league matches alone, versus Newcastle, Sheffield, Edinburgh and Glasgow, as well as paid full-houses against Edinburgh (11+1), Norwich (11+1) and Newcastle (9+3).

Having won the Division Two title, Bristol had to do it all again in 1949, since 'the powers that be' refused to consider them for promotion to the top-flight. Showing they really meant business, the Bulldogs set the pace from the off and literally thundered to another Championship, winning 34 matches and drawing 1, as they finished 10 points clear of runners-up Sheffield. Eric made 40 league appearances in which he amassed $329\frac{1}{2}$ points and also recorded a further four full maximums at Knowle, against Newcastle (twice), Edinburgh and Fleetwood. He also featured in a record-breaking achievement on 7 October, when he recorded 8 points courtesy of four second places, but he was paid for the lot as Bristol hammered Glasgow by the maximum possible score of 70-14. Aside from that, amazingly, he netted 7 other paid maximums against Fleetwood (11+1), Norwich (11+1), Walthamstow (10+2), Glasgow (11+1), Southampton (11+1), Ashfield (10+2) and Sheffield (11+1).

Like all of the Bulldogs in 1949, Eric was pretty useful away from Knowle Stadium, and

it should be remembered that he often rode when he was by no means fully fit. One final interesting feature of the year was the brilliant team-riding partnership he formed alongside Roger Wise, which yielded a staggering total of $688\frac{1}{2}$ race points as Bristol swept to league glory. When the 1950 season came along, the Control Board couldn't do much else but promote the Bulldogs to Division One. But they did it grudgingly, pointing out that they had no riders available for allocation, and stating that the club would have to strengthen itself. Although they went on to finish in the lower half of the table, Bristol were not bottom of the league, that dubious honour went to Harringay, with Birmingham in eighth position, and the Bulldogs one place above in the seventh spot.

Eric was always present, racing in all 32 league matches for 158 points, which wasn't bad at all, especially given the fact that he rode throughout the season still carrying his long-term knee injury. It never rains but it pours, for in addition to Eric's problems, both Billy Hole and Mike Beddoe suffered broken leg bones, and Fred Tuck retired, making it a year to forget in many respects if you were a supporter of Bristol. Obviously scoring was harder at such an exalted level, but Eric did put together plenty of gutsy performances, the high spots being a 10-point return at Birmingham on 27 May, and 9+2 points against the same opposition at Knowle on 28 July.

In 1951, the Bulldogs tracked much the same side as they had the season previously. Despite ending one position higher in sixth place, crowd levels sadly dwindled. Eric managed to attain 141 points from 30 league matches, his best showing being against Belle Vue at Knowle on 25 May, when he gleaned 10 points in a huge 62-22 success. Many of the Bristol riders were, in all probability, as good as they were going to get, and the team was in urgent need of a couple of heat-leaders.

These were not forthcoming, however, and the Bulldogs battled on in 1952, with almost the same set of riders on parade once more. Somehow, they managed to avoid the dreaded bottom position yet again, finishing eighth out of 10 teams, with Eric battling his way to

136 points from 34 matches. The majority of his points were scored at home, where on his day he was capable of beating anyone, as indicated when he recorded tallies of 9+1 against both Belle Vue and Odsal in the early weeks of the campaign.

The 1953 season was very much 'the mixture as before' as far as Bristol were concerned, but Eric's scoring dropped dramatically to 56 points, albeit from only 9 league matches, after his season ended prematurely with a shoulder injury sustained in a challenge match at Southampton on 1 September.

There could be little doubt that all the years of riding when only half fit had taken their toll, but despite this, he was again included in the line-up at the start of 1954, a year which saw the Bulldogs revert back to Division Two racing, after finally propping up the top-flight table in 1953. Eric failed to score in the opening challenge match at Birmingham, but having registered 3 points in the return match at Knowle on 16 April, he was then involved in a track crash, which not only left him nursing a broken arm, but also brought the curtain down on his racing career.

Nevertheless, when Bristol ran open meetings in 1959, and subsequently joined the Provincial League a year later, he was very much involved from the promotional angle. Then, when Knowle Stadium was demolished as a result of being sold for redevelopment, he was the man in charge when the Bulldogs moved to Plymouth for 1961. After a single season at the Devon venue, Eric handed over the reigns to Bernard Curtiss, and was left to reminisce on the many memories of his considerable contribution to Bristol Speedway - the only club he ever rode for.

Competition	Matches	Points
League	73	439
National Trophy	7	54
Provincial Trophy	17	166
ACU Cup	4	42
Coronation Cup	4	27
English Speedway Trophy	6	38
Union Cup	2	10
Challenge	27	179
Mini-Matches	1	3
Bulldogs Total	**141**	**958**

Harold Shepherd was born in London on 5 May 1903, and began his league career with Crystal Palace in 1930, remaining with the club until the end of 1933 when the promotion moved their operation lock, stock and barrel across London to New Cross. During his stint with the Palace, he made his one and only appearance in the prestigious Star Championship final in 1931, but was out of luck on the big occasion, running a third place in his heat, and failing to qualify for the semi-final.

With New Cross, Harry developed into a very good team player and one who ensured that an excellent spirit ran throughout the Old Kent Road side. He stayed put for three years until 1936, also helping out at Provincial League Bristol in the latter season, together with team-mate Roy Dook. At the time, the sport had just returned to the West Country circuit and was managed by Ronnie Greene on behalf of Knowle Greyhound Stadium, with the side participating in the Provincial League. Mr Greene was grateful to New Cross promoter Fred Mockford for the loan of his riders, and Harry duly made his debut in the colours of Bristol in their very first team match, a league fixture at Nottingham on 28 April. It was a great start too, as the side raced to a narrow 34-33 victory, with Harry netting 10 points, and providing excellent support to his skipper Roy Dook, who not only recorded a four-ride maximum, but also established a new track record of 75.36 seconds in the first heat. The opening meeting at Knowle was on 8 May, when Bristol faced Southampton, again in the league, with Harry contributing a valuable 7+2 points as his team collected a 38-32 success.

As the season progressed, he proved to be a steady scorer and was good for a fair share of points wherever he rode. Liverpool came to Knowle on 22 May, and the result was an excellent Bristol win by 41 points to 30, Harry leading from the front with an unbeaten 11+1 points. He must have particularly enjoyed the league visits of the Merseyside team, since when they came again on 31 July, he recorded another paid maximum (11+1) in a 52-19 victory. However, in between, when Liverpool travelled down for a Provincial Trophy match on 26 June, they left with a 40-32 victory under their belts, and only Harry showed any worthwhile form for Bristol, netting 8+1 points.

At the end of the campaign, the Bulldogs, as they had become known in August, only just missed out on the Championship, having to settle for second spot behind Southampton, purely on race points difference, both sides having attained 20 points from the 16-match league programme. Harry appeared in 15 of Bristol's fixtures, scoring a total of 102 points, but crucially, the one meeting he missed was the second home engagement with Southampton on 4 September, when the visitors won 37-35.

In 1937, Fred Mockford joined forces with Ronnie Greene to promote the Bulldogs under the banner of 'The Bristol Motor Sports Ltd', and Harry became a club asset rather than a loaned rider, and he was also made team skipper. It was a well-deserved honour and he responded by continuing, ever-present, to knock up 167 points from 20 matches, as the Bulldogs turned the tables on Southampton, and stormed to the League Championship, finishing 4 points ahead of the Saints.

He was 'Mr Consistency' around the 290-yard Knowle circuit, never scoring less than 7 points, with his best showings being scores of 11 against Southampton, Nottingham and Norwich. On his travels, he did almost as well, the undoubted highlights being 12-point maximums in away wins at Liverpool on 26 April, and Leicester on 6 May. One other performance of note occurred against Liverpool (again) in a Provincial Trophy tie at Knowle on 25 June, when Harry thundered to a brilliant 17 points from 6 starts in a 67-41 success.

Following their elevation to the seven-team Division One, Harry continued with the Bulldogs in 1938, when the team was bolstered by the allocation of Cordy Milne,

Vic Duggan, Morian Hansen and later Bill Clibbett; all of whom joined via Hackney Wick who had reverted to the cheaper running costs of racing in Division Two (as the Provincial League had been renamed). With Cordy Milne on board, Harry went straight to the management and stated that the American should succeed him as captain. This was typical of his sporting nature, and the Bristol fans welcomed the subsequent announcement that Harry would be vice-captain of the side.

It was tough for 'Shep' in the top-flight, but he stuck to the task as only he could, his highest score of a difficult year being 8+1 points in a home league match against Harringay on 22 April. For a second successive season, he remained ever-present throughout the league programme, scoring 77 points from 24 matches as the Bulldogs slumped to the foot of the table, finishing 8 points adrift of sixth placed Harringay.

Following such a disappointing season, there was little surprise when it was subsequently announced that Bristol would be competing in Division Two in 1939. Ex-Hackney boys Cordy Milne, Morian Hansen and Vic Duggan left for pastures new, but Bill Clibbett stayed on, and once again Harry took over the captaincy of the Bulldogs. Happily, he found the points a bit easier to come by, netting a total of 93 from 14 league matches before racing was abandoned due to the outbreak of war.

The high spots of his Division Two campaign were scores of 9+2 against Norwich, and 10 versus Newcastle at Knowle on 23 June and 7 July respectively. By coincidence, his best away performance was also achieving a 10-point haul at the Brough Park home of the Geordie outfit on 3 July. Prior to that, in the National Trophy, he weighed in with a six-ride paid maximum (14+4) as the Bulldogs ran riot to hammer Crystal Palace 83-22 at Knowle on 16 May, and followed it up with 11+1 points from a 65-35 success in the return leg on 27 May.

Perhaps Harry's greatest honour occurred at Knowle Stadium on 14 July, when he proudly skippered England in a Test match against the Dominions, scoring 6½ points, plus 4 bonus when following partner Jim Baylais home. Unfortunately, his side went down to a 63-44 defeat in a meeting run in wet conditions following heavy rain, with the victorious Dominions headed by 18-point maximums from Eric Chitty and Eric Collins, while for good measure, George Pepper weighed in with a tally of 17.

After the hostilities, it was reported that Harry emigrated to Australia, where he established himself as a master builder. He had previously put his building knowledge into practice in this country, and became famous for something other than his fearless riding, when he and his New Cross bossman Fred Mockford invented the speedway starting gate in 1933. It was claimed at the time that the idea was Fred Mockford's and that the 'gate' was constructed and built by Harry, with the early edition looking rather like the ones used today for horse racing. Great oaks, it is said, from little acorns grow, and from that basic idea, the starting gate as it is known and used worldwide today evolved. The wonderful thing about this invention was that all riders started from a stationary position, rather than the previously used haphazard rolling procedure, thus making racing fairer, and track records more accurate.

Competition	Matches	Points
League	11	$24\frac{1}{2}$
Provincial Trophy	9	43
Challenge	6	44
Bulldogs Total	**26**	$111\frac{1}{2}$

Albert David Spencer was actually born in London on 13 May 1908, but taken to Brisbane, Queensland, Australia as a baby. He learned the speedway business down under, before becoming one of the pioneer British riders in 1928. He proved to be a spectacular rider and a class act as he did the rounds of the London circuits that year, prior to being associated with non-league Exeter in 1929.

Bert was then identified with Leicester super in 1930, when he appeared in 10 Northern League matches. He subsequently returned south the following year, joining Plymouth. Still riding for the Devon outfit in 1932, he qualified for the prestigious Star Championship final, when a second place behind Vic Huxley, saw him eliminated before the semi-final stage.

Having spent four seasons based with the Pennycross Stadium outfit, the exciting leg-trailer took a break, before returning with Bristol in 1936. The West Country team were

embarking on their first year as a league team, under the promotion of Knowle Greyhound Stadium, with Ronnie Greene installed as the front man. Having previously ridden in the higher echelons of the National League, Bert arrived at Bristol hoping that a change of circuit and the slightly lower level of the Provincial League would benefit him. However, things didn't work out that way, and he found the 290-yard Knowle circuit very difficult to acclimatise to. He didn't feature in the team's historic first meeting at Nottingham on 28 April, but he was in the line-up for their first home meeting, a Provincial League encounter against Southampton on 8 May. Helped no end by a 12-point maximum from Eric Collins, the homesters ran out winners by a 38-32 scoreline, with Eric's contribution being a tally of 2. Scoring proved hard thereafter, but on 20 July, Bristol raced at Liverpool in the Provincial Trophy, and he enjoyed a tremendous night, netting 10+1 points in a 42-30 victory. His performance included a superb victory over Lancashire-born Tommy Price in heat eleven, which ended the home star's hopes of a maximum on the night.

Although everyone hoped that would kick-start his season, unfortunately it just didn't happen, although it must be said that Bert did try very hard to master the Knowle circuit. In league matches, his best home showing was a 4-point return against Cardiff on 15 May, but as with all the other riders in the meeting, his score was subsequently wiped from the records, when the Welsh side pulled out of the league, citing falling attendances.

Generally, he did fare better away from home, with his top league performance occurring at his old stamping-ground of Plymouth on 7 July, when his 6 points played a vital part in a 37-35 success. A look at the end-of-term figures showed how hard it had been for the Queenslander, with just $24\frac{1}{2}$ points being gleaned from the 11 league matches he participated in.

The Provincial Trophy was a better contest for Bert, and aside from the aforementioned 10+1 points at Liverpool, he also registered tallies of 8 and 7, in home matches against Southampton on 12 June, and Plymouth on 28 August. All in all, it was a tough year for the crowd-pleasing racer, and this could be attributed largely to the tight Bristol track, which understandably wasn't easy for a leg-trailer to adapt to.

He lined-up in the top-flight for Wimbledon in 1937, while also assisting Norwich in the Provincial League, and in a case of déjà vu, he was to represent the same two side's again the following season.

Bert certainly enjoyed his time with the Norfolk club, accumulating 201 points from 23 league matches over the two years, and it seemed like a natural move when he joined the Stars on a full-time basis in 1939. He clearly revelled in the wide-open spaces of the 425-yard raceway at the Firs Stadium, and when the season was curtailed by the outbreak of war, he had knocked up 102 points from 11 league fixtures.

Bert was back at Norwich immediately following the war, having turned down a posting to Glasgow, with Wal Morton making the long trek to Scotland instead. The 1946 season saw him sweep all before him to score 200 league points, which was not only sufficient to head the Stars scoring, but also the entire Northern League. So dominating was he, that he reached the prestigious British Riders' Championship final at Wembley, where he recorded a 5-point tally against many of the leading men in National League circles.

In 1947, the high scoring continued for Norwich, with a haul of 167 points gleaned in the re-titled National League Division Two. He was to spend a further two years with the Stars, and the points continued to flow from his wheels, as he hit league totals of 149 in 1948 and 179 in 1949.

Sadly, the era of the leg-trailer was coming to an end, due partially to changing track surfaces and many debates over tyres, none of which helped these thrilling speed merchants. Bert duly returned to his adopted homeland at the end of his love affair with Norwich, having stuck to this exciting riding style throughout his career, even when things became difficult for these exceptional racers as the 1940s progressed. As showmen, they were without an equal in speedway, and although the sport has moved on, anyone who never saw this brand of racing missed a real treat.

During his time in the saddle, Bert represented Australia in three Test match series versus England (1934, 1938 and 1939), as well as two more in his home country (1934/35 and 1936/37). Continuing with the international theme, he raced for his country against the Provincial League (1937), before being identified in a Dominions race-jacket in two series versus England (1938-39). After retiring from the British scene, he later represented Australia in two more Test series against England in 1949/50 and 1952/53.

Competition	Matches	Points
League	14	$86\frac{1}{2}$
National Trophy	4	18
Provincial Trophy	4	40
Challenge	6	34
Mini-Matches	1	0
Bulldogs Total	**29**	**$178\frac{1}{2}$**

Roland Stobart was born on 26 December 1909, in Aspatria, Cumbria, and was a member of a speedway racing family, his younger brother, Maurice, also being a rider. Rol actually got his first bike in 1928 (a 1926 Cotton), and initially appeared in sand races at Skinburness in both 1929 and 1930. The brothers were well known in the North of England, and Rol was a competitor at Barrow's Holker Street circuit in 1930, a track incidentally that only had a two-foot high safety fence, made of corrugated iron sheets, with sharp points at the top! The following year, he was identified with both Leeds and Preston in the Northen League, and was the driving force behind an idea to stage dirt-track racing at Lonsdale Park, Workington. However, in the event, just one meeting was staged at the venue that season, on 15 August, when a crowd of some 2,000 turned up to see what it was all about.

In 1932, Rol began the season with Preston before being transferred to West Ham where the one and only Johnnie Hoskins was promoter. During a four-year stint with the club, the Cumbrian became a 'film star', assisting in the making of a long forgotten speedway movie, entitled *Money For Speed*, which was made in 1933. Ida Lupino played the main role, but Rol was on hand to take care of all the racing scenes and this was certainly an interesting time for him, especially when he saw himself crash heavily into the safety fence in the final cut.

Happily, he had no memory of this actually happening, and it later transpired that a dummy had been used for the dramatic effect. While at West Ham, Rol also took part in one of Johnnie Hoskins' most famous publicity stunts – 'The Ride to York' – along with team-mate Arthur Atkinson. The idea was that the two of them would recreate legendary highwayman Dick Turpin's ride from London to York. However, Rol just couldn't get to grips with riding a horse, and soon became saddle sore! *The Daily Mirror* gave the stunt huge publicity, and there were many protests about cruelty to the horses for having to make such a long journey. The stunt fizzled out when one of the horses became lame on the second day and the trip was aborted, with both Rol and Arthur Atkinson returning to London by train!

During his first term with West Ham, Rol again rode at the aforementioned Workington circuit, being victorious in the Scratch Race event at the track's first meeting of the year on 14 May. A move across London saw him link with Harringay in 1936, but he was to re-join West Ham later on in the season.

A very busy year followed in 1937, as Rol not only raced for both Bristol and Wimbledon, but he also acted as team manager to Workington in their home challenge matches once he was ruled out of action through injury from mid-July onwards. Looking particularly at his year with the West Country outfit, Knowle Stadium opened for business on 26 March, when a composite side of Bristol and Wimbledon riders defeated New Cross 46-35 in a challenge match, with Rol's efforts yielding 7+1 points. On 9 April, West Ham Reserves were the visitors for another challenge fixture, and the Cumbrian racer enjoyed a terrific night, netting a paid maximum (10+2) in a huge 60-23 Bulldogs victory.

When the league programme got under way, Rol proved to be a most useful points grabber, especially around his home strip, with the highlight being a tally of 11½ against Norwich on 11 June – the half-point occurring in heat eleven, when he and team-mate Roy Dook could not be separated as they flashed across the line together. The match was rather one-sided, with Bristol romping to a 64-18 win, but it must be said that the opposition were severely handicapped, as they turned up without sufficient riders, and were also minus manager Max Grosskreutz. Indeed, home boss-man Ronnie Greene had to lend the unfortunate visitors several men just so the meeting could actually go ahead. Rol also enjoyed the second-half of the meeting, when equalling the time of 33.4 seconds set by the aforementioned Max Grosskreutz a year previously for the two-lap track record (from a rolling start).

Prior to that great night, Rol had raced to a paid maximum (9+3) against Leicester on 30 April, but those points were subsequently removed from the records when the Midlanders closed after only a handful of meetings. Aside from his great showings against Leicester and Norwich, he also weighed in with unbeaten totals of 11+1 points on both occasions that Liverpool visited, plus a score of 10+1 against Southampton.

Generally, he wasn't quite so effective away from home, although he did make some vital contributions; particularly when he plundered 11 points in a 44-39 success at Birmingham on 23 June. Rol seemed to have a penchant for matches against Liverpool, as in the Provincial Trophy, he posted home and away scores of 10+2 and 11 respectively, but

unluckily his season ended abruptly on 13 July, when he crashed in an away Mini-Match versus West Ham Hawks, suffering a dislocated shoulder and a broken arm. This was a cruel blow, since he was showing excellent form, and was comfortably filling the role of a competitive middle-order man cum heat-leader, as emphasized by his league record of 84½ points from just 11 matches.

In 1938, he returned to track action, but Bristol were then a Division One outfit and he struggled to find his form. Having gleaned 5 points from a couple of challenge fixtures, he went on to ride in just 3 league matches for 2 points.

Rol subsequently moved back into the lower division with Newcastle, where he again rode under legendary multi-track promoter Johnnie Hoskins, with brother Maurice alongside as one of his team-mates. The move did him the power of good, as he recovered a lot of his old sparkle to register 99 points from 16 league matches. In addition to Newcastle, he regularly rode at Workington in 1938, until the track closed for good in late July.

Both Stobarts remained with the Geordie side in 1939, and Rol enjoyed a fine time until the premature end of racing due to the war. He recorded 131 league points from 15 meetings to occupy second spot in the club's scoring behind ace Canadian George Pepper.

During the war, Rol served in Africa and the Middle East, and it wasn't until 1948 that he returned to track action with Newcastle; contributing to the Diamonds cause with 25 points from just a handful of league matches.

In 1949, Johnnie Hoskins transferred his Newcastle licence to Ashfield, Glasgow, with the Stobart's accompanying their illustrious boss, plus a number of their riding colleagues to the new Scottish venture. The first meeting at the 355-yard circuit was staged on 19 April, when Rol scored 6 points as the Giants defeated Walthamstow 48-36 in a National League Division Two encounter. Sadly, having gleaned a total of 39 league points, he quit the sport in mid-season, after a crash involving Jack Young had left him with a fractured skull.

Following speedway, Rol ran a light haulage business with his brother, and later moved into the manufacture of agricultural implements.

Competition	Matches	Points
League	15	109
Anniversary Cup	8	59
Challenge	4	23
Mini-Matches	1	2
Bulldogs Total	**28**	**193**

Harold (Harry) William Stock was born in Rainham, Essex on 18 February 1918, and it is certainly an interesting story as to how he acquired the nickname for which he was popularly known. It all came about well before the Second World War when he earned his living doing a milk round, and his cart was pulled by a horse named Nobby. After a while the regular customers began referring to Harry as Nobby, and the name just stuck!

In 1937, Nobby began taking more than a passing interest in speedway, and attended a training school run by Arthur Warwick at Dagenham. Having learned the basics he tried his luck at Hackney Wick, but with riding opportunities few and far between, he began doing various odd jobs for Frank Hodgson, who had broken into the London side in May that year.

With Hackney Wick opting for the cheaper running costs of Division Two racing in 1938, Nobby's persistence was to pay off when he finally made a team place late in the year. He recorded 33 points from 7 league matches and played a part as the Wolves secured the League Championship on race points difference from Norwich.

Furthering his experience, the season also saw him race for Dagenham in the 5-team Sunday Dirt-track League, with the other participating sides being Eastbourne, Romford, Rye House and Smallford. Nobby was to remain at Hackney Wick until the outbreak of war, netting 58 points from 12 matches before the 1939 season was brought to a premature end.

At the beginning of the hostilities, he enlisted and spent seven-and-a-half years serving in France, North Africa and Italy. Whilst in Italy, the speedway bug bit the Essex boy again, and he organized meetings in which he rode on makeshift tracks constructed by fellow soldiers. Programmes were issued for these events, and though they are exceptionally rare, Swindon-based super-fan Geoff Parker has actually got a copy of one in which Nobby is listed as Staff Sergeant H. Stock. The rider-cum-soldier was subsequently present when the Bari track opened, and when the South-East Italian Championships were staged at Trani, Staff Sergeant Stock was the winner in three out of the four contests staged.

Upon his return to the UK in 1947, Nobby discovered he had been allocated to Harringay, whose heat-leader trio were the famous Australians Frank Dolan, plus brothers Vic and Ray Duggan. It was hard work though, because many of the riders who were big stars before the war were racing in the top division, but even so, Nobby accumulated 50 league points from 18 matches, and was considered to have done well enough to be retained.

However, the going got even tougher in 1948, and after 7 league matches, he moved on loan to Division Two side Bristol, having scored just 18 points. The West-Countrymen had lost Mike Beddoe to a serious foot injury in a track crash at Fleetwood, and Nobby knew that a period of racing in a lower division would help his confidence, while also enabling him to earn some cash. In front of 21,000 spectators, he made his debut for the Bulldogs in a league match at Birmingham on 10 July, but in something of an inauspicious start, he netted just a single point as the side went down to a 62-22 hammering. Things quickly began to look up though, and Nobby was to not only prove a valuable points contributor for Bristol, but also a popular teamster. In six out of eight home league matches, he registered tallies of at least 9 points, including three paid-maximum scores of 9+3 against Edinburgh, Newcastle and Fleetwood.

Meanwhile, on the team's travels, he came up trumps with a super unbeaten four-ride showing (11+1) at Middlesbrough on 23 September as the Bulldogs claimed a 45-38 victory. In fact, that success proved vital in the battle for the league title, with the men in orange and black subsequently going on to fill the top spot by 5 clear points from Birmingham. Having scored 109 points from 15 matches, Nobby played a big part in that glory, as he more than covered for Mike Beddoe's absence, and augmented the top-end of the side.

His best night in Bristol colours, however, occurred in an Anniversary Cup match against Glasgow on 6 August, when he revelled in appallingly wet conditions to record a four-ride maximum.

At the close of the season, the Bulldogs supremo Reg Witcomb tried very hard to secure Nobby as a permanent member of his team, but Harringay had taken more than a passing interest in his points plundering while away on loan, and recalled him to their starting line-up for 1949.

He was to be a solid middle-order man for the Racers over the next four seasons, during which time he accumulated 505 points from 124 league meetings, his best year being 1951, when he achieved a 6.39 average. In 1953, Nobby was transferred to Southern League Ipswich for a reported fee of £550, which was certainly a tidy sum in those days, and especially for a rider who was nearing the end of his career. Anyway, he managed to plunder 138 league points for the Witches, a figure that helped them up to third place in the final table, behind Champions Rayleigh, and second placed Exeter.

Remaining with Ipswich in 1954, Nobby's consistency began to tail off, and after netting just 28 league points, he saw out the year with Oxford, prior to retiring to concentrate on business interests. Looking at the career of Nobby Stock, his record at Bristol shines like a beacon. He joined the club when his confidence was at a low ebb, but by the end of the 1948 season he was a confident scorer, being equal to any rider around the Knowle Stadium raceway.

Competition	Matches	Points
League	38	63
National Trophy	4	9
Spring Cup	2	1
Coronation Cup	3	1
Challenge	11	10
Mini-Matches	2	6
Junior League	19	55
Bulldogs Total	**79**	**145**

Born in Bristol in 1927, Jack Summers joined his local speedway club in 1950, the year that the team were promoted to Division One of the National League. It was apparently skipper Billy Hole who introduced the grass-tracker to the Knowle set-up in the first place, and it was indeed a brave decision for Jack to link with a side in the top league.

However, he only had to look to team-mates Dick Bradley and Chris Boss to see that improvement in the higher sphere was possible. Dick had come through the ranks, and although initially expressing doubts about his own ability, he would go on to great things, while Chris had made slow but sure progress, and continued to do so in top-flight racing.

Initially, it was second-half outings for the keen youngster, but his debut for the Bulldogs was to occur much sooner than he or anyone else had expected, when Bristol entertained Wimbledon in the Spring Cup on 21 April. Popular teamster Eric Salmon was out of action after suffering a double collarbone fracture in the previous week's home match,

so Jack was drafted into the side. A crowd of 13,015 turned up for the meeting, and they were fortunate enough to see the Bulldogs romp to a 74-46 victory, with the new team member netting but 1+1 points.

First-team outings were few and far between following that, and Jack's learning curve continued with second-half rides. It is sad to relate that in mid-season, Bristol were suffering from injuries to key riders, and Fred Tuck had retired after completing a dozen league matches. So, when they visited table-toppers Wembley for a National League fixture on 27 July, it was a very much weakened side that reported to the Empire Stadium. Both Mike Beddoe and captain Billy Hole were missing, and with nothing like the guests or the rider replacement rule in those days, the Bulldogs tracked a makeshift side that included Jack. This was some match for him to make his first league appearance in, and before a crowd of 47,000, the Lions raced to a 54-29 success, with Jack contributing 2+2 points to the Bristol total. Sadly, no visiting rider crossed the finishing line first throughout the entire match, but good things were still to come for Jack, when he and partner Chris Boss romped to successive maximums, giving them a 10-2 victory in the Junior League match that followed. It is interesting to note that although Jack was in his first season of speedway racing, this was to be his only appearance in the junior competition all year.

With reference to the main team, he was to represent the Bulldogs in a total of 5 matches and, as if to emphasize just how hard it was, he only accumulated 5 points along the way. Jack's best performance of the campaign occurred in a National Trophy tie at Knowle on 11 August, when he notched 4-2 points from 2 starts in a 66-42 win over Odsal.

There's no doubting it was a difficult first year in the sport, but he had plugged away, and the Bristol faithful held great hopes for him in 1951. However, as happens with many a rider, it was a year when he tended to 'stand still'. His main team outings were still restricted somewhat, but he was a regular performer in the Junior League. The highlights of his year in the competition were two-ride maximums in home matches against Wimbledon on 13 April, and Odsal on 27 July (although the meeting against the Dons was later scrubbed from the records upon the Londoners withdrawal). With a total of 51 points from 18 matches, Jack was certainly equal to the junior riders of any other side, but the league really couldn't be taken seriously, not just because Wimbledon pulled out early, but also due to the failure of New Cross to enter a team in the first place.

For the main Bulldogs outfit, he managed 10 league appearances, as and when required, however, he enjoyed no luck whatsoever and a total of 8 points stressed just how tough Division One racing could be.

It did seem obvious that Jack needed experience at a lower level, but the opportunity to race in either Division Two or the Southern League surprisingly never materialized, and he again attempted to hold down a team place with Bristol in 1952. By and large he managed to achieve that, although it was usually as cover for injured or absent riders. In all, he made 23 league appearances for 50 points, and his best showings at home were against Norwich on 6 June and Odsal on 12 September, with scores of 4+1, and 4+2 respectively. Meanwhile, on the team's travels his best tallies were 4+1 at Wimbledon on 21 April, and 4 at Norwich on

7 June. It could fairly be described as a mixed season for the Bristolian, but at least he got more rides, and wasn't just confined to junior events.

Sadly, the 1953 season was to signal the end of Jack's speedway career. He began the year with an unbeaten 4+2 points from 2 outings in the opening meeting at Knowle on 3 April, when the Bulldogs thrashed Birmingham 74-33, in the first leg of the Inter-City Cup, but he wasn't in the side for the return fixture. He then had three matches in the Coronation Cup, scoring just 1 point at Belle Vue, and having not featured in the team in either the league or the National Trophy, he was finally loaned out to Southern League Plymouth.

It was felt he would do a good job for the Devils, but in the event, he only recorded a couple of points for them, having appeared to have lost his sparkle. He subsequently gave up racing, which was a great pity, and left folk wondering whether he had perhaps remained with Bristol just a bit too long. He did, however, do his level best for the Bulldogs, and it has to be remembered that many of his rides were against some of the very best speedsters in the world.

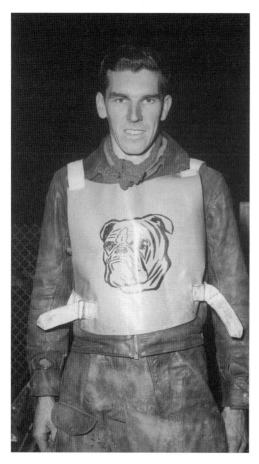

Competition	Matches	Points
League	34	141
National Trophy	8	36
Coronation Cup	16	50
Southern Shield	12	47
Challenge	20	91
Bulldogs Total	**90**	**365**

Edwin Vernon Taylor was born in Perth, Western Australia on 4 April 1927, and as a rider, he was always programmed as Chum. However, in 1960 when Poole began racing in the Provincial League, he was appointed team manager for a few matches, his name appearing as E.V. Taylor, with many supporters simply not realizing that this was actually Chum!

His racing career had begun in his homeland at Claremont in 1949, and in those early days his opponents included Odsal captain Ron Clarke, who was touring Australia at the time. Chum was successful in defeating Ron, which was quite a feat as the Odsal man was one of the leading British riders of the day. So impressed was Clarke that he encouraged Chum to travel to Britain in the furtherance of his career. In 1951, Chum was to make the long journey to these shores

to race in Division Two under Johnnie Hoskins at his Ashfield (Glasgow) venture. It was a bit of a culture shock for the young Aussie though, as he had been used to riding on big circuits like the 641-yard one at Claremont, whereas the Ashfield track was just 355 yards in length.

After limited opportunities with the Scottish club, Chum asked for a move, and was duly snapped up by Division Three side Cardiff. Here, the racing strip was 400-yards long, with an excellent shape and he was to settle in well, recording a total of 59½ league points. Despite sustaining a broken bone in his neck, courtesy of a track spill at Claremont during the Aussie season, Chum returned to the Welsh outfit in 1952, and was to make real progress on his way to a league tally of 252 points.

In 1953, Chum again hoped to represent the Dragons, having enjoyed a sensational season at home, during which, he had beaten the great Jack Young in match races. However, upon arrival on these shores, he found a story doing the rounds that he had requested a transfer to a Division One club. Explaining the situation to co-author Glynn Shailes some years later, Chum stated, 'It wasn't true, I had not asked for a move, but it seemed Cardiff were broke, and wanted the £1,000 transfer fee that I could command. Both West Ham and Bristol had shown an interest in obtaining my services, so I decided to pick Bristol, which was only some 50 miles from my Cardiff home. Looking back, it was a mistake – I had nothing against the Bristol management and fans at all, it was just that the 290-yard Knowle circuit was smaller than anything I'd been used to, whereas West Ham was 440 yards. In the event, while I was at Bristol, I actually scored better away from home, especially in 1953.'

A look at the facts and figures revealed that Chum made his debut for the Bulldogs in a challenge match against the Swedish Tourists on 10 April, when he failed to score in a 56-51 victory. He went on to appear in 14 league matches that season, gleaning 42 points in the process, and emphasizing his comments, just 11 of that total were registered on his home track. Chum's top score at Knowle was 4+1 points against Birmingham, while on the team's travels, his best performance was 7 at Odsal. He even managed to record the lowest total possible in a Coronation Cup match against visiting New Cross on 15 May, when he ended the night with just half-a-point to his name in a thrilling draw. This happened when the ACU Steward was unable to split Chum and Bill Longley of the Rangers as they tore over the finishing line in heat thirteen.

Having not enjoyed the best of years in the colours of Bristol, Chum was determined to be more effective in 1954. At the time of making his decision to stay put, he wasn't aware that the Bulldogs would request a move down to Division Two, but he deserved a slice of luck, and his scoring around the tight Knowle bowl was to prove much better. He remained ever-present over the 20-match league programme, totalling 99 points, of which 43 were scored at home.

His best performance at Knowle was a tally of 9 points against Exeter, while 8+1 was his highest away total, achieved from three rides at Swindon.

At the end of the campaign, Chum returned to Australia, and was to stay down under until resuming his British career with Charlie Knott (senior) at Southampton in 1958.

In all, he was to enjoy four seasons with the Saints, during which he compiled a grand total of 475 league points, and made it through to his one and only World Final in 1960, finishing with a 5-point tally. While with Southampton, Chum was to again ride for Bristol in 1959, scoring 20 points from 3 appearances when Knowle re-opened to the shale sport with a short series of open-licence meetings.

After spending a year in his homeland, Chum hoped to rejoin Southampton in 1963, but having made the long trip over, the Control Board deemed the Saints plenty strong enough anyway, and he was posted off to Oxford. Chum wasn't pleased about this turn of events, and whilst he recorded 105 league points for the Cheetahs, he made it plain that had he known his return to the Saints would be blocked, he would have stayed in Australia.

In 1964, he received a late call from his old boss Charlie Knott to ride for Poole in the Provincial League, and in helping to bolster a mediocre side he netted a total of 124 points.

After missing another season, Chum came back over for a taste of British League racing in 1966, when he linked with Cradley Heath to score 183 points from 33 matches, although in truth, he never really showed his best form.

That was to bring the curtain down on his racing days in this country, although he did return to Britain in 1973, when his son Glyn joined Peterborough. Chum thought perhaps he could gain a team spot too, but sadly it didn't work out, as Glyn moved on to Crewe, while his father suffered a fractured shoulder in a second-half race. It was to be his final ride, and he subsequently went home, leaving his son to race on in the UK.

Competition	Matches	Points
League	29	99
National Trophy	5	10
Provincial League KOC	1	4
Southern Shield	2	3
Challenge	6	6
Mini-Matches	4	18
Bulldogs Total	**47**	**140**

Roy Taylor was a born in Bristol in 1929, and followed in the long tradition of local riders who appeared in the Bulldogs colours. His career began at Knowle in 1953, and there was no doubting that he had all the right attributes as far as the Bristol bosses were concerned. He had a nice tidy style right from the off, and was also pretty nifty when it came to leaving the gate.

Bristol opened their turnstiles to the 1953 season with an Inter-City Cup match against visiting Birmingham on 3 April, when the Bulldogs revealed a mean mood to pile up a huge 74-33 success. Following the main meeting, it was the turn of the juniors to face their counterparts from Birmingham in a mini-match, with Roy representing Bristol, alongside Cliff Cox. Although only run over two heats, the young Bulldogs rode well enough to secure a 7-5 win, with Roy scoring

6 points, courtesy of victory in both races. On 11 April, the Bristol riders made their way up to Birmingham for the return Inter-City match, and again stormed to victory by 59 points to 49. As at Knowle, there was also a mini-match, but this time the junior Bulldogs went down to an 8-4 defeat, with Roy netting all 4 points.

Both Roy and the Bristol management knew that what he needed was plenty of rides, but with the Bulldogs racing amongst the elite in Division One, it was obvious that opportunities would be limited to second-half races, plus the odd mini-match here and there. To help Roy gain vital experience, it was therefore decided to loan him out to Swindon, who were then competing in the Southern League, under new bossman Bill Dutton.

He duly made his debut for the Robins in a league match at St Austell on 16 June, and although Swindon lost 47-37, Roy acquitted himself well to notch 2 points from two outings. He subsequently made his first home appearance for the Robins in a league match against Southampton on 4 July, when he scampered to victory ahead of visiting no.1 Ernie Rawlins in his first ride, before going on to accumulate a total of 6+2 points. He was actually only to ride in one further league match for Swindon that year, and when Norman Parker took over the speedway affairs in 1954, Roy returned to Bristol, who were then operating in Division Two.

Competition for team places was tough, but after making his full club debut in a challenge match at Birmingham on 3 April (when he failed to score), he was to make the most of the chances that came his way to net 13 points from 6 league matches. However, it would surely have been better for both rider and team if Roy had been given an extended run, as it has to be said that a number of the Bulldogs appeared to be just 'going through the motions', believing their places in the side were safe.

Sadly, in June 1955 Bristol were forced to close down due to the low number of spectators frequenting Knowle Stadium. At the time, the Bulldogs had completed 14 league matches, and Roy had appeared in a dozen of them, registering 21 points. He subsequently returned to Swindon in 1956, but with his league appearances limited to just three matches, he understandably seemed to have lost some of his zest for racing.

Roy was to sit out 1957, when the sport was down to just 11 senior tracks, but in 1958, he was back in the Robins nest to score 31 points from four matches in the unfinished Junior League. He also rode in a solitary league match for the senior Swindon side at Norwich on 24 September, but didn't score from 4 rides.

Until 1960, Roy could more or less be said to have been in retirement, but with the formation of the Provincial League, he was happy to again join his old side – the re-born Bristol Bulldogs, who had run a short season of open-licence meetings the previous year.

He soon settled in, becoming a very handy 'back-up' rider to the heat-leader trio of Johnny Hole, Trevor Redmond and Cliff Cox. He contributed some very useful scores along the way, including a wonderful 12-point maximum in a 52-20 league success over Bradford at Knowle on 13 May, and a 10-point tally against Stoke in the following week's home fixture.

Sadly, his season was brought to an abrupt halt when Bristol rode in a league match at Yarmouth on 28 June. In the second heat, Roy smacked into the fence on the fourth bend of the Caister Road circuit, and was taken to hospital with back injuries. His final total for the year was 65 points from 11 matches, which clearly indicated that had he been allowed earlier opportunities, he might have carved out a more than satisfactory career in the sport.

He was to spend the following year out of the saddle, but that wasn't the end of his racing days, as in 1962, Trevor Redmond formed something out of nothing at Neath, and remembering his former team-mate, duly signed Roy to race for his new Welsh Dragons side. The Neath story is one of the most incredible in speedway history, for the side who rode their home matches in little more than a field, were so inspired by Trevor Redmond that they almost won the Provincial League Championship, actually finishing as runners-up to Poole. With a total of 132 league points, it represented Roy's most productive season in speedway, but as had happened to him previously, his home track closed down at the end of the campaign. If only Neath could have enjoyed more support, who is to say what might have happened? The team spirit generated by Trevor Redmond was incredible, and his team could easily have gone one better and won the league title given another year.

The Neath promotion moved to St Austell in 1963, but Roy didn't follow suit, instead hanging up his leathers again – this time for good.

During his time in the saddle, he always gave of his best, particularly for the Bulldogs, after all, he was a Bristol boy through and through.

Competition	Matches	Points
League	91	753½
National Trophy	8	81
British Speedway Cup	9	83
Anniversary Cup	13	139
Spring Cup	6	37
Challenge	22	190
Mini-Matches	1	7
Bulldogs Total	**150**	**1,290½**

Henry George Frederick Tuck was born in Leyton, London on 16 October 1916, but was to spend his entire racing career being known simply as Fred Tuck. At over six feet in height, he was tall for a speedway rider, and with the surname of Tuck, he was quickly nicknamed 'Friar', after the character from the Robin Hood legend.

Aged 15, his father first took him to watch the cinder sport at West Ham, and Fred made up his mind to become a rider himself. By 1935, he had signed a Hammers contract, but there was to be no instant success, so in order to gain some experience, the following year he linked with Provincial League side Plymouth.

In 1937, another move saw him spend the season with Nottingham, and he was happy to remain with the club in 1938. However, having completed their group matches in the English Speedway Trophy, the White City Stadium-based team closed down. Nottingham had also beaten Hackney Wick in the National Trophy, but having shut their doors to the sport, the defeated London outfit were reinstated in the competition! Leeds, who had been running open-licence meeting, subsequently stepped in

to take over Nottingham's league programme, with Fred taking his place in the Yorkshire side.

The final year of pre-war racing saw the lanky racer on the move again, with Stoke being his next port of call. Unfortunately, a lack of support was cited as the reason why the Staffordshire team called it a day after the completion of just eight league matches, although Belle Vue Reserves were on hand to take over their outstanding fixtures. This meant another change of home base for Fred, and as if all that wasn't enough, the season was then curtailed by the outbreak of war.

However, it was during the hostilities that he became a regular competitor in the wartime meetings at Belle Vue, developing into a most able rider. Among his successes was the winning of the All England Best Pairs in 1943, when he was partnered by Canadian ace Eric Chitty.

With the war at an end, Fred was allocated to Odsal for the 1946 season, and he did reasonably well to record 117 league points as the Boomerangs claimed third place in the six-team National League. Despite notching over 100 points, Fred wondered whether or not he was up to the standard of top-flight racing, and although he began the 1947 campaign with Odsal, he put in for a transfer to Bristol, who had entered the newly-formed Division Two.

Having recorded 52 points from 14 league matches for the Yorkshire side, his wish was granted and brought with it a change of fortune in the Bristol camp. The Bulldogs had been having a tough time, mainly because a number of their riders only had limited experience of league racing. Happily, the arrival of Fred Tuck changed all that, following his club debut in a league match at Newcastle on 7 July, when he netted an eight-point tally. By the season's end, he had accumulated 131 league points from just 14 meetings, helping the side to avoid the wooden spoon and occupy sixth position out of the eight participating teams.

Fred's fine team-riding became a regular feature, with his efforts securing many extra points for the Bulldogs cause. Indeed, before the season closed, Bristol had become quite a force at Knowle Stadium, and everyone connected with the team eagerly awaited the beginning of the 1948 campaign. No wonder too, because as soon as the tapes rose, it was obvious that Bristol were literally on fire. They put together a string of most impressive scores, with Fred enjoying his speedway as never before. The Bulldogs raced to the League Championship, taking victory in 23 of their 32 league matches, and 'Friar' topped the side's scoring with exactly 300 points, while his total for all official fixtures (inclusive of National Trophy and British Speedway Cup) was an incredible 469.

So dominant were Bristol that the word around the terraces was 'we should be promoted', and no one could doubt that they deserved to be. Often riding alongside Jack Mountford, the duo formed a particularly potent partnership, which was as good as any in their sphere of competition. Aside from that, Fred also grabbed the Division Two Match Race Championship, when defeating Dick Geary of Fleetwood in the April/May challenge, before losing out to Wilf Jay of Newcastle in June. Another highlight occurred at Poole on 31 May, when Fred and some of his fellow Bulldogs took part in an individual contest for the Silver Trophy. He proved to be in unbeatable form to claim the prize with an immaculate 15-point full-house. Many long-term Poole supporters may well recall the sight of him holding up the trophy and calling to his mother in the stand to 'Come and get it.'

But, despite their success, promotion was not forthcoming for Bristol, and so to prove their class they turned out in 1949, and repeated what they had done the previous season, namely winning the League Championship. As speedway journalist Peter Morrish wrote succinctly 'Bristol made Division Two a one horse race.'

Fred wasn't quite as commanding as he had been in 1948, mainly because of a nasty track accident that saw him sustain a broken jaw. But even so, he still gleaned a total of 247½ league points. To give some idea of the strength of the Bulldogs, his tally was only sufficient for him to finish fifth in the team's scoring!

During the year, Bristol put together some quite amazing scores at Knowle, including the record-breaking 70-14 maximum possible victory over Glasgow on 7 October, when Fred scored the lot (12). After winning the title for a second successive year, the Control Board were left with little alternative than to promote the Bulldogs, and they duly began the following campaign amongst the elite of Division One.

Fred remained on board, although he had given the management notice that he wished to retire from active racing in order to concentrate on his growing business interests. What turned out to be his final appearance for Bristol was a league match at Belle Vue on 17 June, when the homesters ran riot to win 63-21. With 7 points, Fred went out as his side's highest scorer on the night, taking his league total for the year to 75 points from 12 matches.

Everyone was sad to see him go, and he was to be missed, not just for his scoring, but also for being a wonderful team player. Geoff Pymar had been signed from Harringay the week before in order to bolster the team, but in truth, the Bulldogs could have done with both him and Fred riding alongside each other. Officialdom had given Bristol virtually no assistance to strengthen up for the rigours of Division One racing, and as well as Fred's retirement, they had to soldier on when Mike Beddoe and skipper Billy Hole suffered bad knocks, while Eric Salmon raced for the greater part of the season with a brace around an injured knee!

Being so tall, Fred's left leg was almost 'hung out to dry' when he was riding, although his foot was never far from the white line.

A team-mate of his once told of a race involving Fred and Birmingham's Australian star Graham Warren. Looking to drive inside, the powerful Aussie dashed right up to Fred, who hastily withdrew his left leg, claiming after the race that had he not done so, 'the so and so would have slid underneath it!'

Competition	Matches	Points
League	50	373
National Trophy	12	98
Coronation Cup	16	85
Southern Shield	12	101
Challenge	24	145
3 Team Tournament	1	8
Bulldogs Total	**115**	**810**

John Edward Unstead, always known as Jack, was born at Bethnall Green, London on 16 February 1926. His interest in motorcycle racing dated back to his service in the army during the Second World War, when he was a regular and successful competitor in scrambles events.

As a speedway rider, Jack made his debut on the cinders at Rayleigh on 30 April 1949, and in a sensational start, he raced to a 12-point maximum, inspiring the Rockets to a 46-37 win over Exeter in a Division Three encounter. Something else was remarkable too, since Jack's name wasn't even included in the match programme as he had been drafted in so late! The following week against visiting Tamworth, he scored 11 points, again inspiring Rayleigh to victory by 45 points to 37. His dropped point came in the very last heat, when he completely missed the gate, yet fought his way through from the back, and was just inches away from his Tamworth opponent as they flashed across the finishing line.

After such an outstanding beginning, Jack came down to earth somewhat, however, he'd proved he had what was required, and when the Rockets journeyed to Plymouth for a league encounter on 16 June, he dashed to a four-ride full-house, while, just for good measure, he also put up the fastest time of the meeting. A look at the end-of-season statistics

revealed a total of 207 points for the Londoner, which was a mighty fine effort in his first season of activity.

In 1950, with their former skipper Pat Clarke transferred to Oxford, Jack was appointed captain of the Rockets, and celebrated by rising to the top of the side's league scoring with 239 points. Unfortunately, Rayleigh only just avoided the wooden spoon (which went to league newcomers St Austell), having lost several key riders, including the aforementioned Pat Clarke prior to the start of the campaign.

The Essex outfit fared much better in 1951 though, finishing fourth in the ten-team Division Three, with Jack plundering 228 points despite suffering a painful eye injury, which proved slow to heal. By this time, Jack had gained quite a reputation as a tough opponent, who asked for, and took nothing in a race. Not only was he was broad shouldered, but as strong as an ox, and had proved to be among the very best riders in his sphere of racing.

In 1952, Division Three became the Southern League and Jack topped Rayleigh's points chart for a second time with a huge tally of 320, as he skippered his team to the Championship by a clear 10-point margin from runners-up Cardiff.

Having understandably begun to think seriously about a move to a higher level of racing during the Rockets glory year, Jack subsequently joined Division One Bristol for a fee of £1,500 in time for the start of the 1953 season. Many promoters thought the price tag excessive for a Southern League rider, but the West Country club happily shelled out, with promoter George Allen considering it money well spent. Sporting the famous Bulldogs breast-plate, Jack duly lined-up in the opening match of the season: an Inter-City Cup match against Birmingham at Knowle Stadium on 3 April. Bristol were rampant on the night, blasting to a 74-33 success in front of 16,575 spectators, with the new boy netting 6+1 points in a quiet, yet efficient manner.

Jack worked hard to establish himself at Bristol, his wholehearted efforts endearing him to the Knowle regulars, with the league high spots being 12-point maximums against West Ham (17 July) and Norwich (21 August). Life on the road wasn't quite so fruitful though, with 5+2 points representing his best performance at West Ham on 25 August. He did, however, take great pleasure from a Coronation Cup match at a rain-soaked Wimbledon on 18 May, revelling in the conditions to score an unbeaten 12 points as the Bulldogs claimed a 50-34 success. At the end of the season's racing, he had remained ever-present throughout the 16-match league programme, gleaning 90 points, with his final tally actually putting him second in the team's scoring behind Dick Bradley.

Having endured four barren years in the top-flight, Bristol dropped down to Division Two in 1954, and went on to emerge as League Champions. Even though the team was winning, crowds were poor, although one thing that pleased those who attended was undoubtedly the improvement of Jack Unstead.

He again occupied second spot to the brilliant Dick Bradley in the scoring stakes, with plenty of fine riding taking him to a total of 163 points from the full quota of 20 league fixtures. Double-figure returns littered his record for the year, with an unbeaten performance (12 points) against former club Rayleigh at Knowle on 23 July being particularly pleasing.

The 1955 season dawned, but sadly things were no better from the point of view of turnstile numbers, with the upshot being that the Bulldogs shut down in June. At the time, Jack had appeared in all 14 league matches the club had participated in, accumulating 120 points, and was well on course for another marvellous year. However, it didn't take former team Rayleigh long to secure his services, and he was to rack up another 205 points for the Rockets, thereby taking his combined league total to a massive 325 for the year.

Following that, Jack was to remain on board with the Essex club for two full seasons, during which time he recorded 418 league points, prior to moving lock, stock and barrel with the promotion (headed by Vic Gooden) to Poole in 1958.

In his first year as a Pirate, Jack found it hard to master his home circuit, but nevertheless he showed unbounded determination to end the league programme with 90 points to his name. More of the same gutsy performances were produced the following year, when he plundered 136 league points, and finished just 7 points adrift of top man Ray Cresp in the Poole scorechart.

In 1960, Vic Gooden moved his promotion to Ipswich, as the stadium at Poole was sold, with new boss Charlie Knott intending to run Provincial League racing at the venue. Jack was finding the pace of higher-level racing a little hot by this time, and this was reflected in a league tally of 73 points for the season.

Despite finding points difficult to come by, he stayed with the Witches in 1961, but when the opportunity arose to link with Exeter late on in the year, Jack jumped at the chance of taking some rides in the less exhausting Provincial League.

With a fee of £200 changing hands, his transfer to Exeter subsequently became permanent, and Jack was in the Falcons line-up ready for 'tapes-up' in 1962. His club debut occured on 2 April, when Poole visited the sweeping County Ground circuit for a challenge match, and although plagued by mechanical problems, he still managed to attain 6 points in a 45-33 defeat. Exeter then lost 45-32 in another challenge at Cradley Heath, with the Londoner's equipment singing much more sweetly as he collected 12 points from 5 starts. Back at the County Ground two night's later, Jack revealed his true form to land a faultless 12-point maximum as the Falcons raced to a 44-34 success in the second leg of the challenge against Cradley Heath. He then rounded off a good evening by beating Ivor Brown in his Scratch Race heat, before going on to win the final from team-mate Len Silver.

The story of Jack Unstead was to come to a tragic end on Friday 13 April, when he was killed while guesting for his old club Ipswich in a challenge match against Southampton at Foxhall Heath. Having scored 2 points from his opening ride, the fatal accident happened in the fifth heat, when Jack unfortunately clipped partner Colin Gooddy's rear wheel, before being thrown through the safety fence into a lamp standard. Sadly, he was already dead when the track staff reached him, and so a man with a big heart was taken from the sport of speedway.

Competition	Matches	Points
League	155	853½
National Trophy	16	162
British Speedway Cup	12	80
Anniversary Cup	15	125
Spring Cup	6	30
Challenge	38	247
Mini-Matches	3	5
4 Team Tournament	1	6
Bulldogs Total	**246**	**1,508½**

Stanley Roy Wise was born in Swindon, Wiltshire on 25 November 1912, and throughout his speedway career, he was always known as Roger. He was one of many West Country boys who joined Bristol in 1946, when a series of open-licence meetings were staged at Knowle Stadium. His arrival in the Bulldogs camp came following trials at West Ham, and although he wasn't associated with the London side for long, the record books for the year show that R.Wise recorded 1 point in league matches.

Roger wasn't without motorcycling experience, since before the Second World War he was an outstanding competitor on the grass-track circuits, winning trophies in many events, especially at the Kingsdown circuit, near Swindon, which was actually run by his family.

Anyway, having linked with Bristol, he made his debut for the club in what was actually their first post-war team match on 2 August, netting 8 points in a 62-45 success over Birmingham. He went on to appear in 11 of the challenge matches held that year, and with a total of 77 points to his name, had done much to impress the management and supporters alike. Riding with great enthusiasm, his performances included a return of 10+4 points against the

Northern League Stars on 4 October, and 10+2 verses Sheffield on 18 October.

In 1947, the Bulldogs began racing in Division Two of the National League, and although they initially took time to settle on their own track, they did get better as the season progressed, eventually knocking up several big wins on the tight 290-yard raceway. Although Roger wasn't in the team at the start of the campaign, he soon claimed a regular spot to score 124 points from 26 league matches - this representing a fine effort in his first full season of racing. Roger put in some terrific performances along the way, none more so than when he raced to a paid maximum (11+1) against Newcastle at Knowle on 26 September. There was also one away match of particular note, which occurred at Wigan on 18 October. Prior to the meeting, Bristol had tasted defeat in each and every one of their previous 20 away matches in all competitions over the course of the season, yet somehow pulled off a shock 43-41 victory, led by a fabulous 11-point tally from Roger.

Due to their poor form on the road, the Bulldogs had been struggling to avoid the wooden spoon, and their surprise win certainly helped to that end. As it was, the final table showed them occupying sixth place out of eight sides, with 2 points separating them from both Wigan and Glasgow. Had the West-Countrymen lost the match at Wigan, they still wouldn't have finished bottom, however, as their race points difference was far superior to that of Glasgow's.

Roger lined-up with the Bulldogs right from the off in 1948, and in stark contrast to the previous year, the men in orange and black carried all before them as they swept to the league title by a 5 point margin from nearest challengers Birmingham.

In Fred Tuck, Billy Hole, Eric Salmon, Jack Mountford and Roger, Bristol possessed a power-packed top-end, which led the side to a 100 per cent record at home, and no less than 7 away successes on their Championship charge. Indeed, the Bulldogs top men became renowned throughout the sport for their team-riding, which especially delighted the huge crowds that flocked through the Knowle turnstiles every week. Remaining ever-present throughout the 32 league fixtures, Roger's contribution was 229 points, and included paid maximums against Edinburgh (9+3), Newcastle (11+1) and Middlesbrough (10+2).

With Bristol's application for Division One racing subsequently turned down by the Speedway Control Board, the team begrudgingly faced another season at the lower level in 1949. If proof were needed that they should have been promoted, then the Bulldogs certainly provided it as they stormed to a successive league title by 10 clear points. They were an awesome unit around Knowle, exemplified by the maximum 70-14 thrashing of Glasgow on 7 October, and a 68-16 mauling of Norwich the following week.

Roger was again ever-present during the long 44-match league programme, recording a massive 359 points to occupy third position in the side's scoring, behind Billy Hole and Jack Mountford. His scoring included full 12-point maximums at home against both Glasgow (in the aforementioned meeting) and Ashfield. However, he was just as able on the away tracks too, notching four-ride full houses at Coventry and Walthamstow (twice).

Overdue as it was, Bristol were finally promoted to Division One in 1950, with the Control Board stating they would have to strengthen their team themselves. This, they tried to do, but apart from the acquisition of Geoff Pymar from Harringay, no other rider seemed keen to travel west, leaving the Bulldogs to soldier on as best as they could. Like several of his team-mates, Roger found the going hard, and whilst Bristol were a tough nut to crack at home, they did struggle away from Knowle. However, they did manage to finish in seventh position out of the nine participating sides in the final league table, with Roger netting $88\frac{1}{2}$ points from 29 matches, the high spot of his year being a tally of 8 against West Ham in a home match on 2 June.

Unfortunately, things went badly wrong for Roger in 1951, when a loss of confidence meant him losing his team place; so much so that he only actually rode in a single match for the Bulldogs, scoring 1+1 points in a home encounter with Wimbledon on 13 April.

Thankfully though, Oxford, who had been promoted to Division Two for 1951, saw a rider of Roger's experience as being just what they needed to add a bit of 'bite' to their line-up, having lost key riders through injury. Slowly, but surely, he regained his zest for racing to end the campaign with a total of 95 league points for the Cheetahs.

Roger returned to Bristol for the 1952 seasons, riding mainly as a reserve, but his year was blighted when he was involved in a nasty track spill in the first of two league visits to West Ham on 27 May. The accident happened in heat thirteen, when Roger was unable to avoid the rear wheel of home man Reg Reeves, and was subsequently taken to hospital suffering from head injuries and concussion.

After a spell on the sidelines, he did return to the Bristol side, but was never the same rider again, and understandably retired at the close of the campaign, having registered 52 points from 23 league matches.

He was to be greatly missed by the Bristol fans who regarded him as something of a folk hero. To emphasise this, an interesting tale was once told about Roger by one of his former team-mates. It centred around an unavoidable delay in racing, when he went to the track microphone and began chatting to the crowd, happening to mention at one point

that he loved toffees. The story goes that a further delay then ensued whilst the track was cleared of a mass of toffees, which had been sent showering down by the supporters for this most popular of Bulldogs!

In addition to being a fine all-round motorcyclist, Roger was also both a coach builder and a master baker. Certainly, people living in the Swindon and Highworth areas some years ago will remember that he and his family ran a business making superb cakes that were enjoyed by many.

In 1962, Roger returned to speedway as team manager of his local club Swindon, but it wasn't a very successful time as the Robins finished just one place off the foot of the National League table. After just one season he resigned, leaving his old pal Bob Jones to take over the duties once again, having previously managed the side from 1956-61.